# Meditation

Searching for the Real You

First published by O Books, 2009
O Books is an imprint of John Hunt Publishing Ltd., The Bothy, Deershot Lodge, Park Lane, Ropley,
Hants, SO24 0BE, UK
office1@o-books.net
www.o-books.net

Distribution in:

UK and Europe
Orca Book Services
orders@orcabookservices.co.uk
Tel: 01202 665432 Fax: 01202 666219
Int. code (44)

USA and Canada
NBN
custserv@nbnbooks.com
Tel: 1 800 462 6420 Fax: 1 800 338 4550

Australia and New Zealand
Brumby Books
sales@brumbybooks.com.au
Tel: 61 3 9761 5535 Fax: 61 3 9761 7095

Far East (offices in Singapore, Thailand,
Hong Kong, Taiwan)
Pansing Distribution Pte Ltd
kemal@pansing.com
Tel: 65 6319 9939 Fax: 65 6462 5761

South Africa
Alternative Books
altbook@peterhyde.co.za
Tel: 021 555 4027 Fax: 021 447 1430

Text copyright Dada Jyotirupananda 2008

Design: Stuart Davies

ISBN: 978 1 84694 219 8

A CIP catalogue record for this book is available
from the British Library.

Printed in the UK by CPI Antony Rowe

O Books operates a distinctive and ethical publishing philosophy in
all areas of its business, from its global network of authors to
production and worldwide distribution.
This book is produced on FSC certified stock, within ISO14001
standards. The printer plants sufficient trees each year through
the Woodland Trust to absorb the level of emitted carbon in
its production.

# Meditation

## Searching for the Real You

## Dada Jyotirupananda

BOOKS

Winchester, UK
Washington, USA

# CONTENTS

# INTRODUCTION

"In the living being there is a thirst for limitlessness."
Shrii Shrii Anandamurti

In my mid 20s, I met a well known natural healer, Dr. John Christopher. His practices included a technique called iridology which says that by examining the irises of a person eyes, one can discern illnesses or injuries that the patient may have had.

I made an appointment with him and after a short conversation he spent 15 or 20 minutes looking at my eyes, and writing down my symptoms.

Upon finishing he looked at me and said: "You do meditation, don't you?"

I said, in a tone of surprise and mild questioning: "Yes...?"

He said: "I thought so. Because without meditation, you would have had a severe nervous breakdown by now."

I was more than a little surprised. How often would someone my age have such a problem, I wondered. And in my family there were no such cases that I knew of. But later, reflecting upon my life before and after meditation, which I had taken up two or three years earlier, I felt that he was correct.

Some years earlier (before I had started meditating), at the start of my university life, I met a fellow named Caylor. Our initial meeting made me feel: "We've known each other before." I'd never had an experience like that (unless I really HAD known someone before).

As our friendship developed, our conversations often led us toward questions that were far more penetrating than anything we dealt with in the classroom. I don't recall that we ever planned the direction of our conversations, but by the end of many of our sessions, I desired to find deeper insights into life, and was left wondering how to find some sort of permanent security or stability in a world that seemed far from secure.

At the end of the school year I returned to my hometown and worked in a petrol station most of that summer. By the time we met again in the autumn, Caylor had gone through some intense mind experiments, starting with LSD and graduating to something called Yoga. I had only a vague idea of what yoga was and as far as I could recall, it had never touched my life or that of anyone I knew.

Caylor was now talking a lot about yoga, meditation, and related things. (In fact, one of the early things I learned from Caylor was that yoga practices include meditation. Yoga is far more than just physical exercises.) I was fascinated at this new way of seeing the world. I learned that with yoga I could guide myself simply by the way I thought about life. My mind could do more than the normal dreaming and undirected thinking that I was used to. One could perhaps recall past lives, communicate with others mentally (telepathically) or control one's own health by will power.

Thus through our regular meetings, a new world was opening up to me. I came to understand that there is much more to a full life than simply high grades, a pretty girlfriend and a good job. I slowly started to understand that there were mysteries of the universe that were far beyond what science or philosophy usually addressed.

These stories describe the two reasons that initially lead me to practice meditation. On the one hand I needed to find some sort of 'center' inside myself. That is, I needed to feel a sense of inner stability and security that would help me understand how to get on with my life.

On the other hand I had a sense that there were many secrets of the universe that could be known to me, and of course to others, if we could only find the vehicle to get us there.

Years later I realized that these two reasons converge at one point: the desire to find fulfillment in life, which can also be called eternal happiness, or an unending peace of mind.

So after some years of seeking, I found a path that helped me move toward this deep sense of peace. Thus I could fulfill my first need, to find a secure center in myself. And the calmness that one can gain from meditation helped to make my mind clear enough to understand at least some of the mysteries of life that had intrigued me up till then (and indeed, some of these mysteries still intrigue me now).

These mysteries were questions such as: is there a purpose for life? Is there an afterlife? Is there a heaven and hell for us to run toward or away from? Is there a higher being, a universal consciousness (what may be called God or Brahma or Allah among many other names)? If so, why does it sometimes seem absent from our lives; why does it seem to hide from us?

Thus I had two reasons for taking up meditation. These reasons, I believe, are similar to why other people also pursue meditation. In the early stages a person is likely to approach meditation to improve their condition in life. One person may want to de-stress. Someone else may want to improve their concentration. Or gain more self-confidence. Or improve their memory.

On a more subtle level, which might be called the second stage, one may want to know the meaning of life. Or to find peace of mind, a level of fulfillment that we may call "the peace that passeth all understanding."

All of these reasons for practicing meditation are valid and attainable.

I had started meditation with both stages in mind.

On the one hand, I did have a lot of stress. Dr. Christopher apparently saw healing lines in my eyes, which indicated that I was, at that time, 'de-stressing.' I didn't really know where the stress came from and perhaps it's not important to think about that now. Suffice to say that too much tension, distractions, lack of self-confidence, a wandering mind and other factors had prevented me from feeling much happiness or sense of success.

When I first took up meditation I wasn't intending to avoid a nervous breakdown, but somewhere in my sub-conscience I probably knew that I needed some tool to help me get hold of life, get in touch with life.

As for the second stage, I felt that meditation would guide my mind in a direction that would help me explore these mysteries and then I could develop a deeper sense of myself and of the universe.

As I read various books on yoga, I started to sense that the separate beings of my self and 'it' – that is, everything that was not 'me' – were not so separate after all.

Although the unfathomably large physical universe was certainly 'outside' of me, there was another sense of the universe, that is, as one song says, 'deeper than the deepest sea.' And this, I intuitively felt, was part of me.

Sometimes I felt that I could almost grasp these fantastic ideas. At that stage in my life, though, they were only ideas. Fascinating, intriguing, exciting, yes, but so far, just ideas. However, I was learning that these ideas could become real.

Finally I started to practice meditation. The catalyst that motivated me to practice meditation was unexpected, even five minutes before it happened. I was sitting in a cafeteria on campus with Gus, a good friend of mine who had been practicing meditation for perhaps a year. I was in a bit of a coffee-daze (not an unusual state for me in those days) and grumbling a bit about life, as was also not unusual for me. Gus reminded me that there was a meditation course starting on campus that week. It was the last course before the start of the summer holidays. He said that if I joined it and then started meditating, I would have the whole summer to practice meditation with few distractions.

Gus's comment cut through my self-imposed fog and helped me see a light at the end of my tunnel of confusion. For a minute or so I reflected on the idea that I too could actually DO meditation instead of just philosophizing about it. So I said, "Yes, of course," and from that moment I never looked back to my previous lifestyle.

A few days later I started the course. I still remember walking home after that first evening class and saying to myself: "I'm going to start meditation soon and I will do it for the rest of my life." That was quite a daring statement considering that I had never been able to continue with anything that became too demanding; but something inside me knew that with meditation I would persevere. And after all these years I'm still practicing it every day.

As I noted, there are many valid, reasons why people start to meditate. My experience tells me that if you do persist with a meditation practice, you'll sooner or later seek answers to the deeper questions even if you didn't start to meditate for any spiritual or esoteric reasons.

This book will provide you with tools that can help you to meditate, whatever your purpose is for taking up meditation. It can also help you to gain a stronger commitment to a regular meditation practice.

Also, consider that this is a book to enjoy! Learn a lot about how to meditate, about yoga exercises and related practices. Learn how to be healthy through your own efforts and how to adopt a code of conduct that will see you through life's difficulties and as well, will help guide you to the deepest fulfillment.

From this book you may also learn that success in meditation depends on your will power, your determination, and your desire to use the tools of meditation seriously and regularly. You may see that meditation (along with related practices and principles that we discuss in this book) is a vehicle that can help you reach a stage of fulfillment and inner peace beyond your furthest expectations.

Thus you may find that the rewards that come from a regular

meditation practice are both here and now as well as 'out of this world.'

If we can learn how to use these tools of meditation, which ultimately can lead us toward the most profound understanding of life, while along the way giving us many advantages, such as more self-control, and more joy in life, then we can be successful in every way, partly because we'll have a deeper understanding of what 'success' means.

# Chapter 1

# FIRST STEPS TOWARD SPIRITUALITY

'As long as I can conceive something better than myself I cannot
be easy unless I am striving to bring it in to existence or
clearing the way for it.'
— George Bernard Shaw

"There is in the living being a thirst for limitlessness."
— Shrii Shrii Anandamurti

"We are all one child spinning through Mother Sky."
— A saying of the Shawnee nation

When I first went to the circus as a young boy, everything was
new and strange. I tried to find a way to place this new
experience into what I already knew about life. The lights, the
music, the smells, the colors of the tents and the costumes were
all enchanting, but they were also frightening.

I still well remember the tightrope and the trapeze artists.
High above us mortals on our wooden seats, they seemed to defy
both ground and death: jumping, twisting, turning, flipping
while exchanging star-struck smiles and dramatic grimaces.

Each performer displayed an exquisitely delicate, precise
balance and a sure strength.

Years later I understood that the joy and daring these
performers exhibited came from many hours of practice, practice
and more practice... in other words, discipline.

I used to think of discipline as restrictive, something that
required a somber face and straight shoulders. My present view

5

is more like that of Stephen Covey, who notes that one who is disciplined is "disciple to a philosophy...a set of principles (or) values (or) to an overriding purpose... or a person who represents that goal."

*Webster's Dictionary* says it is 'training that corrects, moulds or perfects the mental faculties or moral character.'

So now I see discipline as a mental attitude that will help me to reach a goal. I can be cheerful and eager and still be disciplined. Discipline adds guidelines and structure to the quest for a goal.

We need discipline of course to accomplish anything meaningful. When we hear about someone who has 'struck it rich' in some venture, or who has acquired some great honor, we may say, "Well, someone had to get it. Lucky for them." However, while this 'good fortune' may seem to have 'just happened', it is usually the result of discipline, of pursuing their goal in a methodical way.

When I was a teenager one classmate of mine was the son of a millionaire; millionaires were then a rare breed to us. We all envied Marc's good fortune. It seemed he had a life of ease and opportunity awaiting him.

So it was odd to us other kids that his father made him take a job to earn his pocket money.

The father apparently understood that so-called good fortune comes to those who prepare for it.

In my mid-20s I worked in a small natural foods store. One of our popular products was home-made baked goods by Barbara, a woman who'd started baking for a local store in her hometown. Somehow her food was popular locally and in a short time her baked goods were a national craze among health food freaks. I sometimes would think, "I wish I could bake like her." But more important would have been for me to learn about her hard work, perseverance and determination to succeed.

Each of us must adapt discipline to suit our situation and our nature. Isaac Asimov, for example, became a successful writer with his unwavering habit of writing from 8am to 5pm daily. A friend of mine, also a successful writer, writes whenever he has time, with no set schedule. But he always meets his deadlines. These two writers have different work styles, but they both have a deep sense of commitment to their work.

The wondrous conquest of heights by the acrobats, and the opportunities available to a rich man's son may be favorite dreams for many of us. However, as Benjamin Franklin said, "One who waits upon fortune is never sure of a dinner." We need something more than just desire or a good idea to get what we want in life.

Spiritual practice offers us the chance to conquer heights and opportunities that will make circuses, riches or any other quest seem mundane. Success in spiritual practice, however, depends on the same quality as success in athletics, commerce, science or the arts: discipline.

The author Joseph Conrad notes: "I don't like work... but I like what is in work — the chance to find yourself. Your own reality — for yourself, not for others – which no other (person) can ever know."

Thus work, or self-discipline, is not an end in itself, but necessary in order to progress in life.

In the yogic worldview, life, the universe and, yes, everything, is in constant movement. Our mundane life is marked by constant change. This change takes many forms. A loved one dies, a job opportunity appears, we find a new friend, break up with our partner, graduate from university. Change or movement is the law of life. The table in our room, the book we're holding and the carpet on our floor seem solid and stable. However, on a subatomic level they are in constant movement. This constant change in life is also evident from the changing use of these things. We may use a table for writing or for eating or for holding our TV. A year ago, the table may have been part of a tree in a forest far from our home. A year from now, a fire may reduce it to ashes.

Other movements in our life are more obvious: the cars speeding along the streets, our changing social relations and the swirl of thoughts and feelings inside us. When I was younger, I sometimes found this constant change confusing, and as I gazed at this whirl of life I wondered when – and how – I could find something steady to hold onto.

Later I learned about yoga and felt it could be a steadying influence. It seemed that some people, through the ages, had found truths that went beyond the transitory nature of our normal perceptions. I was excited to think that I, too, could perhaps find these truths and find a direction in my life. We will discuss these ideas in this book.

To take up a yogic lifestyle is to take up a spiritual practice. A 'spiritual practice' is a system that helps us to experience higher truths in our own life. According to Swami Vivekananda, "Yoga is the science that helps us to attain these perceptions (of higher truth)." And though it may not be the only science to help us in this way, it is, according to my own experience and study, a most effective system for achieving this end.

A word about *spirituality* is useful here. It is an awareness or experience of ultimate or universal truths. Is it also, in the words of Anandamurti, a highly respected 20th century spiritual teacher, "a never-ending movement from imperfection to perfection."

Discipline is important for spiritual practice because in the area of spirituality we can achieve nothing useful without a sense of mental balance and inner harmony.

This may seem ironic to many readers. We often come to a meditation or yoga course because we want to find mental balance and harmony. So you may well ask: "If I need to have it, where do I find it? What good is meditation if I need these things before I even start?"

One does not need to have perfect mental balance, inner

harmony or discipline before starting meditation, but a little of it definitely helps.

In my university days, when I started meditation, I didn't have much inner harmony. Long before taking my first meditation course, I had read that meditation involves concentration. I then read some books with concentration exercises that I thought might help me in yoga and in my daily life. I still remember one exercise, where I sat in a quiet, dark room, lit a candle and was supposed to stare at it for a long time. The book said that a deeper awareness would result from that practice. However, although I was completely alone that night, with no external distractions, I could not concentrate for more than a few seconds. I experienced similar results with other exercises I tried.

It was only after I learned a technique of meditation from a teacher that I felt a breakthrough in my ability to concentrate. I'm sure there are several reasons why I was able to meditate after this course. Part of the reason, I think, was because a qualified teacher had validated my 'right' and ability to do meditation.

I was also confident that what I had learned would be useful to me. Thus, I had an incentive to continue the practice. As well, I felt an inner resonance with the mantra, which, I believe, helped me to focus my mind. In chapter five, we will talk in depth about mantras.

My earlier failures to concentrate were soon far behind me as I now found that I could sit still for the prescribed amount of time with little or no problem. My previous difficulties with the candle exercise were far behind me. Part of my motivation came from my first meeting with my teacher; his vibrancy and self-assurance helped me to realize that meditation was important for me. His support for me confirmed that I could meditate. I knew I would be more successful if I kept a regular schedule. I told myself I would ignore any time pressures. No matter how 'scattered' my mind might feel, I decided to sit and meditate for at least 15 minutes twice a day.

My mind soon settled into this routine and I have had no trouble continuing with my meditation since then, though I now meditate for considerably longer periods of time.

My determination to succeed came from a sense of inner discipline, a certain amount of mental balance and a desire for harmony. I had very little of these qualities before starting my first meditation course, but I had a desire to attain more. This desire was, I think, the water that allowed the tiny seeds of balance and discipline to blossom and grow inside me.

## Our Three Lives

"As you live, believe in life! Always human beings will live and progress to greater, broader and fuller life. The only possible death is to lose belief in this truth simply because the great end comes slowly, because time is long."
— W.E.B. Dubois

We human beings live three lives at once. We live physical, mental and spiritual lives. Long term success and happiness depends on a balance among these three. The beauty and quality of a hand-made carpet depends on a subtle blending of strength, texture and colors. Similarly, the inner beauty of human beings depends on an even subtler blending of body, mind and spirit. If we ignore even one of these factors, our life will be out of balance.

A carpet may satisfy us for a while, but after some time we will want something better. In life too, although we can be satisfied with a basic existence, most of us want to attain a better, fuller life than we have at the moment.

What, then, is a fulfilled, fully developed, functional human being like? Is this someone who is happy with their job and family and does not feel much worry in the world? Is it someone who does not see the doctor much because they are rarely sick, and can sleep at night, having had a full and satisfying day?

Of course, for basic survival, our physical, mental and

spiritual lives do not have equal importance. Life will go on even if we don't reflect on spiritual questions, such as where we came from, why we are here or where we are going. Answering these profound questions will not put more food on the table, or pay the bills. We first need physical security.

Security, both physical and social, is the minimum base you need before you can start to search for inner fulfillment. Ironically, even people who say they are content with what they have in the world, who do have physical and social security, often feel 'something' is missing. Sooner or later many start to wonder, "Why am I doing all this? Is there something I'm missing as I rush around all day just to pass my exams, pay my mortgage, or keep up with my friends?" These doubts will begin to vanish when you start moving toward your spiritual center.

What do people look like or act like, who have found this center, or who are at least making an active effort to find it?

In general, I see such people as physically healthy and practicing a form of mental discipline, such as meditation. This helps them to cut through the confusions of mundane life. If this type of person is a student, they will probably try to learn something that enables them to help others or to help the world at large. If they are in the working world, they may have a type of job that gives scope to help others or to help the world. This person will spend part of every day involved in a spiritual practice, such as meditation and will also actively take care of their own physical health. Their life is becoming integrated. 'Integrated' in this context means an effort to maintain physical and mental health while actively pursuing spiritual wisdom.

Integrity is wholeness. A person is whole who takes care of the needs of each part of herself. Integrity also means that a person thinks, says and does the same thing. When they make a commitment, they will do their best to fulfill it and if this fails they will make no excuses. If they see others are not keeping their commitments, this person of integrity will have strength of character to help them improve themselves.

Wholeness involves working on all three parts of life so that our body, mind and spirit can work together. Such practices as yoga exercises, a healthy diet and cleanliness help to reduce the poor concentration and sicknesses plaguing so many of us. We are learning to control our senses, rather than be controlled by them. These practices help us to maintain our physical health and mental balance.

Meditation plays an important role in such a person's life. Through meditation one learns that there is more to life than 'just getting by.' Swami Vishnudevananda says: "The goal of life is to achieve, while still alive, a state free from death, pain, sorrow, old age, disease and rebirth.... Everyone needs to experience the truth within; only then will all doubts vanish and all miseries disappear... Yoga... declares that this truth can be experienced."

Our model person may not yet have experienced the absolute truth in life, but they have had a taste of it. This person knows it is there to find if one has the patience and perseverance to continue the journey.

Is this person, though, just a model, an ideal created in my mind? No, she (or he) is you, but perhaps just a bit farther along the path than you are right now.

We may be able to envision their good fortune if we take a glance at the opposite type of person.

Dr. Andrew Weil tells the story of Mr. Shinichiro Terayama, formerly a physicist and management consultant in his native Japan. For many years Shin's job kept him on call 24 hours a day. He slept little, drank ten to twenty cups of coffee daily and had a poor diet. After living like this for some years, he developed kidney cancer. He went through the standard treatment and though the cancer was checked the quality of his life kept deteriorating. Once he even dreamt that he attended his own funeral.

All this made Shin realize that he had to make some drastic changes in his lifestyle. He left the hospital and decided to seek alternative therapy so he could become involved in the process of curing himself. The next day at home Shin woke up and, thanks to his new attitude, soon saw life as 'unbearably beautiful.' God seemed to be everywhere. He later realized that he had created his own cancer. Now Shin has vigorous health and is an accomplished cellist and a counselor of cancer patients. Weil emphasizes that the quality of Shin's life did not improve so much due to the fact that he recovered from cancer, but because he had undergone a 'psycho-spiritual transformation.'

---

### Give it a Chance

As well as a sense of discipline, we also need determination and patience. In fact, these may well be the two main ingredients of discipline. While we do need some help or guidance on this spiritual journey, as we do on pretty much any journey in life, we also need to find our own way to some degree.

The following story indicates how going through our own struggles or difficulties is ultimately a liberating experience.

A man found a cocoon of an emperor moth. He took it home so that he could watch the moth come out of the cocoon.

On the day a small opening appeared, he sat and watched the moth for several hours as the moth struggled to force the body through that little hole. Then it seemed to stop making any progress. It appeared as if it had gotten as far as it could and it could go no farther. It just seemed to be stuck.

Then the man, in his kindness, decided to help the moth, so he took a pair of scissors and snipped off the remaining bit of the cocoon. The moth then emerged

---

easily. But it had a swollen body and small, shriveled wings.

The man continued to watch the moth because he expected that, at any moment, the wings would enlarge and expand to be able to support the body, which would contract in time. Neither happened!

In fact, the little moth spent the rest of its life crawling around with a swollen body and shriveled wings. It never was able to fly.

What the man in his kindness and haste did not understand was that the restricting cocoon and the struggle required for the moth to get through the tiny opening was the way of forcing fluid from the body of the moth into its wings so that it would be ready for flight once it achieved its freedom from the cocoon.

Freedom and flight would only come after the struggle. By depriving the moth of a struggle, he deprived the moth of health.

Sometimes struggles are exactly what we need in our life.

If we were to go through our life without any obstacles, we would be crippled. We would not be as strong as we could have been.

Give every opportunity a chance.

## The Whole Me, Working Together

The obvious question now is: how can I become like our ideal woman or man, or like the transformed Shin? How can I create balance and harmony between my body, mind and spirit? In order to do so, we need to understand the relationship among these three aspects of our nature. They are not independent components, like the various parts of a car. The radio may function independently of the wheels or the windshield, which doesn't think much about the needs of the fenders. But if a human has one part out of balance, it affects his whole being.

We have no mechanical instruments to measure the relationship between the body, mind and spirit. We therefore have to use our intuition, experience and our reasoning to perceive the relationship among the three.

Philosophers have pondered this subject for thousands of years. European thought on this topic dates back at least to the time of Plato. Plato believed in an immortal soul, but saw it as distinct from the body, although affected by it.

In the 17$^{th}$ century, Descartes thought the mind and body could interact but that there was a clear distinction between them. Mind did not pervade throughout the universe, but existed in individuals. God was the supreme example of the mind.

Later Spinoza proposed a theory of 'psycho-physical parallelism.' He said God possessed infinite attributes, but mind and matter were the only ones known to humans. Humans are composed of a substance which manifests itself in different ways, such as through a physical body and a mind.

Variations and refinements of these three views exist today in European philosophy.

The yogic view is that the body, mind and spirit not only co-exist but also interact with and interpenetrate each other. Medical evidence supports this view. The placebo effect as well as hypochondria shows a clear correlation between the mind and body. In both cases, what we think or believe creates a physical response. Homeopathy seems to cure the body at least in part by creating awareness in the mind of the need to adjust or refine itself. Many physical scientists now accept that the thoughts of a person who observes an experiment has an effect on the results.

The physical and psychological sciences have as yet paid little attention to the spiritual aspect of life.

How can we know if the spirit does interact with or interpenetrate the body and mind? Experience and intuition are the main tools to help us here.

Ralph Waldo Emerson said: "All goes to show that the soul in man is not an organ but animates and exercises all organs. It is not a function, like the power of memory... but uses these as hands and feet. It is not a faculty, but a light. It is the... master of the intellect and will. It is the background of our being..."

Carl Jung suggested a way for us to understand this connection of mind, body and spirit: "Life, if lived with complete devotion, brings an intuition of the Self, the individual being."

Dr. Jean Houston, of the Foundation for Mind Research, noted that: "I firmly believe that all human beings have access to extraordinary energies and powers. Judging from accounts of mystical experience, heightened creativity or exceptional performance by athletes and artists, we harbor a greater life than we know. There we go beyond those limited and limiting patterns of body, emotions, volition, and understanding that have been keeping us in dry-dock. Instead we become available to our capacity for a larger life in body, mind, and spirit. In this state we know great torrents of delight."

One can best understand this connection through direct experience. Meditation is a highly effective method of attaining such an understanding.

There is a corollary to this relationship of the body, mind and spirit: the apparently separate lives of all beings are part of a larger whole. Dr. Boris Podolsky, in his *Psychiatric Handbook* observes: "The minds of all people have a common origin."

Annie Besant adds: "The notion that our little life is a separate, independent unit, fighting for its own hand against countless separate independent units, is a delusion of the most tormenting kind. So long as we thus see the world and life, peace broods far off on an inaccessible pinnacle. When we feel and know that all

Selves are one, then peace of mind is ours without any fear of loss."

The three aspects of a person's nature create one unified whole; they are interdependent because a person needs all three in order to express her complete self. A human cannot express spirituality without a body. The mind also cannot function in isolation. It acts as a link between the body and spirit. It also connects the individual and the rest of the world, sharing and receiving knowledge with others.

One of the main purposes of this book is to help us to understand how to put our 'three natures' together and use them affectively.

## The Goal of Meditation and of Life

'Ignorance is Bliss' they say. Not true. It may be pleasant not to know some things. You may be content to leave the electricity bill unopened on the kitchen table. However, after a few weeks, when your lights, TV and refrigerator stop working, your 'bliss' may also come to an abrupt end.

Although this example may be extreme, I suspect we all experience times in our own life where we accept fleeting happiness as the norm.

As a student, I accepted that I was poor at math and science and did little to try to improve. I did not see them as part of my future life. Later I understood that my poor math skills represented a larger problem. I was lazy when it came to learning difficult subjects. I had no desire to struggle with such things. If I had tackled this deeper problem, I would have achieved more during my student days, not just in the classroom, but in every aspect of my life.

A more widespread problem than lack of ambition or foresight is stress. There is medical evidence to suggest that much of our physical disease is connected to mental stress.

The developed mind of the human being seems to be the

reason we have so many mental complexes, including stress, as well as such things as fear, hatred and anger. The mind, however, also enables us to feel such fine emotions as love, a sense of community, pure peace and happiness.

Each of us wants to succeed. We often link success to very tangible factors such as a job, a car, or a marriage partner. However, while these things can measure some types of success, they do nothing to measure inner peace and happiness. These tangible things can add to personal happiness but they cannot create happiness.

Some admirable qualities are of course related to success in the world: hard work, discipline, responsibility, team spirit, higher education, self-reliance and more. But for every story of how hard work or education helped bring success to someone we also hear of someone else who just cannot lose weight, who goes to the therapist every week (for how many years now?) or who is on their second or third marriage.

We can also find people with these admirable qualities who suffer emotionally. Stephen Covey quotes an associate: "...Sometimes I wonder if what I'm doing will make any difference in the long run. I'd really like to think there was meaning in my life, that somehow things were different because I was here."

I think we all want to make a difference in life, to leave some mark and to know that someone cares about us. My father tried to leave his mark by working to support his family and get his children off to a good start in life. After spending years at this endeavor, his reward was a heart attack. And while I was surprised at his illness, I was more surprised to see that many people just accepted it as a norm: you work, you get old, you get sick. I didn't want my life to be so 'normal' so I started thinking there must be something missing from this system.

While I wanted to keep my vision of a nice house, family, career, etc, I also decided I should peek behind the curtain that was till then at the boundary of my life. I wondered if there was something beyond that boundary that I hadn't yet noticed.

At the age of 19 or 20 I was not afraid of a heart attack, mortgage payments or losing my job. I did, however, think that life could be more fulfilling if I knew why I was here and if there was some reason, some purpose. No need to throw the house away and live in the forests, or, like Diogenes, wander through the streets looking for an honest person. But I did think that if I could at least gain an understanding it would help me see everything in a new light.

As life goes on some of us realize that possibilities exist that we have not yet found. Take a chance; look a bit further than you are used to doing.

The writer, Zora Neale Hurston said: "Mama exhorted her children at every opportunity to 'jump at the Sun'. We might not land on the sun, but at least we would get off the ground."

In yogic terms this could be stated as reaching for our highest goal, which would be a spiritual goal. The yogic attitude to life is that humans all have an essential nature. In fact all living beings have their own essential nature. There are two aspects to this nature of ours: our personal nature and our nature as a member of the human race. To understand our true nature is called self-knowledge.

The Sanskrit word that describes 'self-knowledge' is *Dharma*. The root of the word Dharma means 'to hold.' The meaning has thus become 'knowing one's true nature, one's essential properties.' It is also defined as: 'the basic principles of cosmic or individual existence.'

For example: we know the dharma of fire is to burn. If something seems to be a fire but it merely illuminates, we can call it light, but not fire. The dharma of plants is to be immobile, to take vitality from the earth and food from the air and in turn to create food.

Fire may cook food for us; it, may also burn down a forest or light a cigarette, though not in my house. Although these actions may result from its ability to burn, the actions themselves are not its basic property.

So, what is the dharma of humans? To make war, money, love? To conquer and populate the world? To carry on tradition?

These are all human activities but they are not the essential nature of human beings. The dharma or essential nature of humans is to seek permanent happiness, peace or fulfillment. When anyone makes dharma their priority in life they gain more self-control, more inner strength to do what they need to do. Self-control can help you to study, work or maintain friendships. It can also help you to develop your inner or spiritual life.

Some people ask me what value there is in developing an inner or spiritual life. They say that we need a healthy society, economic security and health. Let God take care of those other things. This proposal sounds simple and easy. Many people, like Covey's associate, however, have economic security, but still wonder what purpose their life is serving. All my experience in life shows me that we need something more than money can buy in order to gain a sense of fulfillment in life.

As American humorist Kin Hubbard noted: "It is pretty hard to tell what does bring happiness; poverty and wealth have both failed."

If we analyze ourselves deeply, we realize that everything we do has the goal of helping us find happiness and peace of mind. Ironically, due to lack of clear thinking, we divert our minds with quick pleasures, mistaking them for long-lasting happiness.

I think many of us assume that if our studies or careers and families are fruitful, then we have found success. But after attaining these things, how do we feel? Are we fully satisfied?

Worldly success is meaningful, no doubt. However, if you put all your energy in that direction I see two downsides. Mundane success is temporary and depends on factors you may not be able to control. A politician may do very good work for his constituents. However, an economic crash may cause the voters to lose faith in him. He is out of a job, due to something beyond his control. A student with an honors degree may find they just cannot get a job: there are too many people in the same field.

Such failures may not be so bad if the person in question has a secure sense of their identity. If, however, you identify very much with your work, or with some particular status, you may feel that you, not just your efforts, are a failure.

There is another downside to focusing only on the material side of life. People who try to excel in the world are often not happy with only partial success. The media is full of stories of people who become ill, get divorced or become corrupted in their all-out drive to succeed. In worst-case scenarios, when seeming success turns to failure, suicide follows.

In these cases of so-called failure, people suffer because they identify themselves with something temporary. Jobs, fame, money, a good house, etc., may be important. We each deserve this type of security, no doubt. It would, however, make good sense to connect ourselves with something more permanent, something not subject to divorce, addiction, heart attacks and the like.

If we always seek happiness from things outside ourselves, something will be missing in our lives. The happiness that comes from getting a new car, a new lover or the autograph of a famous pop star, may be tangible, but it may not last long. If we have inner happiness then we can face difficulties with a sense of peace.

**Meditation and Social Service: Two halves of Self-Realization**
by Kristin Kaoveri Weber, from www.ru.org

Before I started to meditate I had some preconceived notions. It seemed like a good thing to do: to sit quietly and contemplate the peace within, to find one's center, to focus on the infinite. But it also seemed like something for quiet, low-key people: you know, meditative types. I did not see myself in that category. I was outspoken and noisy, and very interested in social action, especially women's issues. So I had another bias against meditation: maybe it was just an escape from reality. Perhaps quiet meditative people were selfish and only concerned with their own spirituality, not with working towards social justice and equality.

Meditation also seemed like a ploy to keep people from fighting exploitation. Haven't the disenfranchised always been placated with religion? "Pray to God and things will get better. Be quiet, look inside." I didn't want to be quiet; I wanted to change the world.

My previous ideas about meditation were not unfounded. Certainly the monk-in-the-cave image has been perpetuated in the West. But after I got over some of my biases and started to meditate (and to understand more clearly the concepts of Tantra, the Indian spiritual tradition which emphasizes the development of human vigor both through meditation and through confrontation of difficult external conditions) I began to see that true spiritual progress is when the internal and the external move together. When we do the internal work of meditation, and we use the strength it gives us to serve our societies, then we have progress. For thousands of years, some spiritual aspirants have chosen to retreat from the world, to caves or ashrams, for the sake of spiritual realization. But the greatest spiritual teachers have never advocated such paths.

"The purpose of our life is certainly about helping others," said the Dalai Lama, "It must be positive. . . Whatever way we can make a small contribution, that's what's important, that's our responsibility." Meditation helps us connect with the universal consciousness, "the One", as some teachers have called it. It helps us to see the unity of all things. And when we begin to sense that unity, we start to feel compelled to make life better for other people and for animals and the earth. If everything is part of the same "One", then the idea of retreating from the world to connect with the universal consciousness doesn't make sense.

The spiritual teacher Shrii Shrii Anandamurti said:

"Do you require the help of a mirror to see your wrist-watch on your wrist? No, you will never do that. Likewise, you need not go to the Himalayas in search of God, who is hidden in your own 'I-ness'. Living in the world, put forth your entire self for the service of society, and then you will attain God."

Meditation is the vehicle by which we purify our body and mind. If everything is part of "the One," and meditation helps us to see this idea more clearly, then meditation will also lead us towards connecting with others: humans, plants, animals, and the earth. We begin to realize that we can't get to our goal of self-realization alone. We have the responsibility of bringing the rest of creation along with us.

As we chip away at our ego and self-interest, feelings of

love start to rise. That love, that open warm feeling you get in the center of your chest when you hold a baby or pet a kitten or nurture a houseplant back to life, that's what meditation cultivates.

While meditation creates that feeling from the inside, it's caring for the baby, kitten or plant that feeds it from the outside. In order for the process to work, both the internal and the external forces of love have to be working on the body and mind simultaneously. This is why it is essential to combine social service with spiritual practice.

I remember when I first felt my fourth chakra (or the "yogic heart" as it's sometimes called) really open up. I had organized a vegetarian dinner to raise money for a children's school in the Dominican Republic. I spent three days cooking, but I managed to get some sleep and do some meditation during the preparation. On the day of the dinner, I had to walk to the store to get some forgotten lemons. I was tired, but as I stepped out into the sunlight I was overwhelmed by an explosion of joy in my chest. I felt like singing and dancing my way to the supermarket. I saw in the trees and clouds the radiant pulsing joy of life and I couldn't help smiling at everyone I passed. It is in these moments, that we feel heaven resides on earth.

## Off the Roller Coaster

You can begin your journey toward wisdom and inner strength with very few accessories. You need, first, the desire to reach this goal. Regardless of the technique you use, you can start with the idea of expanding your view of life. Try to understand that we must base success and happiness on a deep sense of personal peace and harmony.

I meet many people who are busy with their careers or

education, their families and other responsibilities. Throughout their lives, though, they seem to be wondering if there isn't a way off this roller coaster of happiness/sadness, pain/pleasure, excitement/boredom. Is there not something more than this, somewhere?

When I was a new student of yoga I once had a conversation with a thoughtful friend of mine. With my newfound confidence, I said that through meditation we could find a permanent sense of peace and satisfaction. She countered, "But that would be so boring."

I had never had much inner peace at all, so I had trouble holding up my part of the argument. Much later I realized we both wanted the same thing but just had different perspectives on what happiness is.

In one way she was right. Imagine that every movie is thrilling, your city has a park on every corner, every meal you eat is excellent and you always have enough money for all your needs.

This certainly could be very boring. Why? If everything was predictable, there would be no difficulty or struggle in life. As you lived year after year of unvaried satisfaction, you would become so contented you would develop the ambition and drive of a cow.

While a Midas or a Rockefeller can come close to this type of life, they would also be very bored by it.

In fact, there is much research showing that wealth gives very little real happiness in the long run.

Professor Alan Krueger of Princeton University says:

"Money does not play a significant role in day-to-day happiness. It certainly can buy things, but things do not usually address most of the troubles people experience in daily life — concerns about their children, problems in intimate relationships and stressful aspects of their jobs."

Where, then, does permanent peace or happiness exist?

It exists inside us. The world will always provide a mixture of pain and pleasure. If we measure ourselves on how things are going at work or at school, or on the stock market or with the neighbors, we will never find deep or lasting fulfillment. These things are always changing, always subject to myriad factors we cannot control.

And though life is always changing, this is not tragic. Stephen Covey suggests one way to resolve the worries we have when we don't feel we are able to control what is going on around us. He introduced an idea he calls 'circles of concern and circles of influence.'

Covey says that within our circle of concern there may be things over which we have no real control. Positive people will focus most of their time and energy on their circle of influence, on things they can do something about. Their energy, he says, is positive, enlarging and magnifying. Their circle of influence increases as they use their positive attitude and energy to resolve the problems they can resolve.

We do have control over how we look at the world. Is your cup half empty or half full? Even tragedy can be seen from various viewpoints. While a robbery or a beating is tragic, it can also be an impetus for the neighborhood people to talk together, figure out the problem and have a safer street.

Spiritual knowledge can help your cup, that is, your view of life, to become much more than half full. When you first start looking for spiritual knowledge your circle of influence may be small. It might be just big enough for you to read a book or two on yoga and take a weekly class. If you continue with the class and reading, you may, after some weeks or months, learn a technique of meditation from the teacher. This new knowledge will give you a wider circle of influence. You can now take the time, independent of any class, to do meditation. As you learn more lessons of meditation (discussed later in this book) you will gain more influence over your spiritual development.

According to my experience, this is a gradual process. A goal of perfect peace and complete self-control takes a long time to achieve. Let your circle of influence expand in a steady, natural way.

## Movement towards the Goal

As you think, so you become. This is basic to human nature. Of course we cannot always take this literally. Rather, if we want to get somewhere, we need to plan and work toward that goal. Years ago, when I was living in a yoga center in Seattle, in the USA, a man came to our door who had visited our center some years before. We had a pleasant conversation for awhile. Then out of nowhere he mentioned that he was a perfectly realized spiritual master. His actions and his general demeanor, in my opinion were not those of such a person. Although I didn't talk to him for very long after that, my impression was that at some point in his life he had decided to act and talk as he imagined a true master would be. And it appeared to me that in doing that continuously he eventually got it into his mind that he was that sort of person. But I could not see any spirituality in him. He was not, in my opinion, walking the walk, regardless of what he was talking about.

He may have gained a certain sense of security for a while. I doubt, though, that this self-image he had was able to help him make much progress in life, as I'm sure this image was not his true self.

Anyone you choose to substitute for yourself will limit you, even if the person has accomplished much more than you have. That model person does not have the same challenges or responsibilities as you, so you need to find your own way toward success. That model person has used their own capabilities to solve her own problems. She or he is not better than you, just different.

If you want to move toward a certain goal, you need to have

a vision of the goal in your mind. Yoga can help you ascertain the most reasonable goals for yourself. As you use yoga to move toward these goals, it can help you develop a mature personality. It can also help you clarify your vision of what you want in life. Yoga may not help you become as rich or famous as your favorite pop star, but it can help you to become more of who you are.

Meditation teaches that the best way to clarify your vision of what you need is to think of yourself as a complete person. In a few words, I'd say: see yourself as a person who has inner strength and a strong sense of responsibility.

Yoga has existed as a formal practice for many thousands of years. It first became systematized as a spiritual science called *Tantra*. We will discuss this in more detail in chapter two. The word Tantra means to expand, or to remove dullness and inertia from our life. Teachers of Tantra appreciate phrases such as 'be all you can be.' They see that most of us use only a small fraction of our capabilities. Today, while many of us are trained to solve technical or scientific problems, we need to learn how to solve personal, moral or social problems. As we expand our vistas and try to understand our inner self, I believe we can resolve many problems, in the world or in us.

Some obvious questions are: Why is it so important to understand my inner self? What is my inner self? How do I find it? Meditation is the key to answering these questions. Regular practice of meditation helps you envision a spiritual goal in your life. A spiritual goal leads to mental expansion. It gives us a broader perspective on our motivations in life. Many people try to solve their personal problems using only the information in front of their eyes. However, if we can look 'behind our eyes', into our deeper nature, our deeper motivations, we can resolve our problems in a more satisfactory way.

An overbearing person, for example, may decide he needs to change his behavior. One logical thing for him to do would be to ask fewer questions. However, a superficial change like this may not help him get to the root of why he's overbearing in the first place. He also needs to replace the habit (of talking) with something else. The human mind, as well as nature, abhors a vacuum and so we always want to express something. Regular meditation will help this person get to the root of the problem. It will also help him to replace the habit with productive, positive action.

If you want to develop a broader view of life, to gain a better understanding of your motivations and needs, then choose a goal that allows your mind to reflect on the meaning of life.

The purpose of this book is to show a method of living that will help us to grow in a balanced way on all three levels: physical, mental and spiritual.

Many people are aware of what they need to maintain their physical health: good food, sleep, exercise, warmth, for example. Fewer people know how to maintain their mental health. A healthy mind needs, among other things, a purpose in life, a sense of community and friendship and some challenges to enable it to keep growing.

Still fewer people are aware of how to keep their spiritual self healthy. This may be because few people seem to know how to sense or perceive their spiritual self. Dr. Andrew Weil says our spiritual self "is the source of life and power, without which material forms are non-living husks. It interpenetrates matter but is itself non-material. (It is) that central mystery that connects us to all creation."

Yoga can help us find and know our spiritual self. Swami Vivekananda notes: "Our minds have become externalized and have lost sight of the fine motions inside. If we can begin to feel them we can begin to control them."

The mind and body are vehicles that help us find our 'fine motions' inside. However, if the body or mind are unhealthy or out of balance, then it will be difficult for us to sense our spiritual self. Yoga solves this problem by attending to the needs of both our body and mind. In this book you will find exercises, practices and systems to help you create vitality in both your body and mind. You can then learn to gain control over your whole being and progress towards subtler, more expanded levels of awareness.

## How to Get There

I want to add a little more about Tantra (which is practiced daily by the author and editors of this book).

Tantra is a spiritual tradition which started in India several thousand years ago. The system contains detailed instructions on how to develop and maintain physical and mental health and vigor. The main goal of Tantra is how to find spiritual elevation.

Most teachers emphasize the practical aspects, although Tantra has a broad philosophical base. Meditation is an important part of Tantra. Central to the teachings of Tantra is the attitude that we can overcome all difficulties, whether personal or social. Though some of the practices of Tantra, such as meditation, are introspective and thus personal, most teachers of Tantra encourage active participation in the world. As noted above, we will discuss Tantra in depth in chapter two.

Tantric practices developed over a long period of time and are based on a deep understanding of human nature. They take into account the nature of different types of people, such as intellectuals, warriors or farmers. They also deal with fundamental human motivations. Besides our basic human instincts (eating, sleeping, sex and fear), many other, subtler, motivations are addressed: why do we live in society, why do we help or hurt others, why do we search for things outside our immediate experience. Why do we need love and how do we find love?

Through meditation and other tantric practices we can find answers to these questions. As we expand our understanding of human life, our personality also develops. We learn how to maintain our physical health and rejuvenate our body when needed. . We also learn how to make more effective use of our time and to use more of the latent capacity of our minds.

The methods of Tantra have always been taught free of charge. Tantra, then, is not influenced by what is trendy, new, quick or easy. Tantric teachers do not listen to just what the student wants ('the customer is always right.') but rather to what they need. A hairdresser, for example, is glad to give you what you want, for a price. Those of us working on the other side of the scalp — inside — give you what is necessary for your development, if you want fulfillment in life.

Those who practice Tantra gradually learn to understand their inner motivations and psychic complexes. A broad range of practices — physical, mental and spiritual — may be taught, to help the student on several levels. As the student progresses, the teacher can 'fine tune' the practices to suit the individual's needs. The teacher is always ready to provide guidance, but the student must have the desire for such guidance.

A typical program for a student might include meditation, yogic exercises and a suitable diet. Individual problems, such as weight, physical or mental stress, back pain, etc., can be helped through the regular practice of yogic exercises.

All of these points will be discussed in detail later in this book.

## The Individual and Society
(People) do less than they ought, unless they do all that they can.
— Thomas Carlyle

Many persons have a wrong idea of what constitutes true happiness. It is not attained through self-gratification but through fidelity to a worthy purpose.
— Helen Keller

Some of the changes meditation can bring about in a person's life include increased self-control, inner peace, happiness, clarity of mind, improved health and the development of all aspects of the personality.

But what is the purpose of all this?

Humans are social beings. In a spiritual sense, what is good for one is good for all. Peace, happiness, justice and a sense of well-being are what we all want. As we expand our views and understanding of life, through meditation, we learn to use more of our natural abilities. We can also gradually become aware of our kinship with all life.

Some time ago I was at an international conference on human habitation, along with several of my fellow teachers. Throughout the two week conference people asked us how meditation could help solve the problems of society.

We explained that the most basic human needs are food, clothing and health. After satisfying these needs, people want peace and justice.

Peace has little or nothing to do with treaties between governments or with disarmament or with the United Nations. One cannot guarantee what one does not have. Today few people — whether world leaders or regular folks — appear to have inner peace. So the question arises: how can you plant a garden of peace throughout the world when even one seed of peace has not taken root in your own heart and mind?

If we regularly practice meditation, the seed of inner peace and universalism will slowly sprout in each of us. Mental illness, isolation, anger and greed will be weeded out of our consciousness and fall by the wayside.

As your personality becomes more balanced, your thoughts, words and actions will become integrated. This new integrity may cause your friends and associates to wonder what has happened to you. At first they may feel confusion, but I suspect they will appreciate your new self.

Your new integrity and feelings of kinship may lead you to

take the initiative to help others. This may take the form of social service to the poor, sick or disabled. It might also involve active work to change society in our efforts to make peace and justice available to everyone. You will find the type of service that is attractive to you. And no doubt, you will find others like yourself.

Dr. Hans Selye, a renowned researcher on stress, summarized his work by saying that a happy life is the result of making contributions, of having meaningful projects that contribute to the lives of others.

Meditation is first and foremost a vehicle for self-development. However, world peace and solving all of our social problems is also an essential aspect of our goal in meditation.

## People Who Deeply Pursued Personal Development

People learn meditation for a variety of reasons. Some want occult powers. Some want health, happiness, friends or mental strength. One of my students wanted to learn how to control his wife. (I told him that when we have self-control the question of controlling others becomes unimportant.)

Most reasons for learning meditation are valid. Even if your goal is self-realization, still you need to develop your character and your sense of social responsibility along the way. Just as a mathematician must learn addition and subtraction before learning calculus, we must take life step by step.

Mathematicians have objective tools for knowing if they are learning what they should be learning.

In the process of character and personality development, we also have tools for self-analysis.

Ben Franklin developed a system of 13 virtues for personal development. He worked on one point every week and on Saturday he would reflect on his week's progress in relation to that point. These points included justice, moderation, cleanliness and humility, among others.

Andrew Weil gives us an example of another system for self-analysis and personality development. Mari Jean Ferguson had faced years of hypertension and other illnesses. A steady dose of drugs helped her maintain some degree of health. However, slowly she started to think there must be a way off the roller coaster of illness, doctors and drugs. She then went through a period of reviewing and analyzing her life and personality. She saw that many of her problems related to her desire to control everything around her. She taught herself to just relax and let life take its natural course. Soon after this, many of her health problems disappeared.

By the end of this book, you will have learned a series of steps for personal development. For these steps to be effective, it is important for you to be very honest with yourself. I have been practicing self-analysis for more than thirty years and I have learned there is no 'right' or 'wrong' answer in this work. Rather, the most important step is to know that I am honest when I answer each question. Without this honesty I can learn little from self-analysis.

If you want to improve yourself, it helps to have someone with whom you can discuss your 'performance' in trying to improve. Choose someone you think has the ability to help you. You may find your best friends are not always willing to point out your shortcomings. It may also be that they are not trained or perceptive enough to analyze your personal development. We grow very little from hearing how good we are doing.

Diogenes once said: "No man is hurt but by himself." (The same is true for women.)

## Spiritual Development and Yourself
"The journey of a thousand miles starts with but one step."

In my view, meditation and self-development are synonymous.

The yogic or meditation system has been developing over

several millennia. No student can expect to understand it all in one glance. Don't set a time limit. Learn at your own speed, not at the speed you think someone else is learning. Take the first step and see where it leads. Besides reading this book you might consult a qualified teacher if you wish and move along with these ideas at whatever pace is comfortable for you.

I have found that people can only be successful in meditation if they move at their own speed. No robots are welcome here. What is important to you may not be important to others, even to your best friend.

I remember one of the first books I read on yoga. The author was a saintly person with much experience in meditation. He often talked about entering deep states of meditation where he would sit and contemplate eternal truths for hours at a time. It seemed so easy and natural to him. I was just starting to experiment with meditation. No matter how hard I tried I could not find even a drop of what he seemed to be feeling. Nor could I sit in the yogic posture for more than a fraction of the time he sat. I was both frustrated and envious.

Years later I understood that he had reached his level of 'skill' by years of hard, sincere effort. Somehow he had never mentioned this point in his book.

With all the qualifiers I've just made I want to add one more. As you go through this book, do not pick out just what seems easiest. Also choose what is most useful. Meditation is the most essential practice herein. It is basic to everything else in the long run. Granted, it does not appeal to everyone in the beginning. However, if you look for challenges, for something that stretches your present boundaries a little bit, you'll find more ways to grow.

Complete success in meditation will take a long time. But there are many 'small successes' along the way that will reaffirm that you are on a most special path.

Chapter 2

# TANTRA: A WAY FORWARD

"A universal religion, unrelated to the times and unfettered by
ruling circumstances, is a desideratum to be realized, no one
knows when."
— D.N. Bose, H. Haldar

The practices discussed in this book derive from the ancient
spiritual science of *Tantra*. Tantra, a Sanskrit word, means
expansion of the mind toward unlimited knowledge. It also
means 'loom', indicating Tantra was like a loom that wove all the
aspects of spirituality together into a complete pattern. It is a
system of knowledge and practice that relates to both the
spiritual and material aspects of human life. Just as a physical
science has several components, including for example, mathe-
matical formulae, laboratory research, symbols, etc., so Tantra is
also made up of several components. The main ones are: 1)
practices, such as meditation and yoga, 2) philosophy and 3)
guidelines for social and spiritual conduct

The people who developed Tantra were searching for ultimate
truth. They wanted to develop a system that would be accessible
to anyone desiring to learn about spirituality. Earlier systems for
spiritual development were open only to a privileged few. While
developing Tantra, the teachers knew, however, that they were
dealing with imperfect human beings who were plagued by
myriad weaknesses. So they developed practices that would
initially help students to gain self-control. Once a person has
attained a certain amount of self-control they can take up more
serious and intense practices of Tantra. Although initial practices
may vary from teacher to teacher, they generally include basic

meditation, yogic exercises known as asanas and guidelines relating to diet, hygiene and equanimity of mind.

We each have three 'bodies', as mentioned in chapter one: the physical, mental and spiritual. Teachers of Tantra devised methods to develop each of these three bodies. The ultimate goal is complete fulfillment as a person. Along the way these practices help us to gain inner harmony, which includes clarity of thought and self control. We also gain outer harmony, including better relations with others and increased effectiveness in our work or studies.

Tantric teachers have evolved many techniques to help us improve and maintain our overall health and well-being. These techniques are discussed in detail in later chapters.

For physical health, Tantra recommends several factors. One factor is a diet that is good for both the body and mind. Periodic fasting, which gives the stomach a chance to rest, and which also helps to strengthen the will power, is another technique. Yogic exercises – called *asanas* – regulate the glands, nerves and inner organs. The regular practice of asanas is very beneficial to both our body and mind.

For mental health, Tantra developed a series of guidelines called *Yama* and *Niyama* which deal with self control and the regulation of our social behavior. They help us reach a state where negative tendencies do not affect our minds. They also help to develop our mental strength and lead to more harmonious social relationships.

Spiritual health is attained through meditation. Physical and mental health are both prerequisites for spiritual health. Through meditation we can understand our true nature and attain self-control and self-motivation.

A brief history of Tantra is useful here.

The oldest known religious practices are found in the *Vedas*, which are the earliest spiritual scriptures from India, and which form the philosophical base of Hinduism. The Vedic civilization sprang up about 15,000 years ago and flourished in India and other parts of Asia for about 10,000 years. Although the Vedic civilization developed intellectually, their spiritual knowledge was not passed on in a systematic way. Despite theories and philosophy, an effective system of spiritual practice was lacking.

'Veda' means knowledge. Today the Vedas are collected in several volumes. There is much wisdom in these books. The following verse, still quoted today, is an example of the Vedic sense of community:

"Let us move together, let us sing together, let us come to know our minds together. Let us share like sages of the past so that all people together may enjoy the universe. Let us unite our intentions and let our hearts be inseparable. Let our minds be as one mind. As we truly come to know one another we become One."

These thoughts are noble and universal in outlook. Yet scholars comment that Vedic practices were time consuming, ritualistic and difficult for the common people to grasp. Thus with the passage of time, the study of Vedic practices became the domain of priests and scholars. They laid down rigid criteria about who could practice the Vedic teachings and when.

Tantra, which developed independently of Vedic teaching, became popular as people found its practices more accessible.

We do not know the origin of Tantra. It evolved gradually. Tantric teachers or 'researchers' built on the knowledge and experience of their fellow Tantrics. Various Tantric practitioners gradually systematized the teachings, adding, generation by generation, newer elements, or refining existing practices. Tantra is not a 'finished product.' Even today Tantric masters continue to redefine and modernize the teachings.

Tantric teachings can be considered universal in at least two ways. First is that the practices and philosophy are designed to help the student to expand their perception to encompass the whole universe.

38

Secondly, the practices are for anyone and everyone.

Tantric teachings are not tied to any particular culture, nation or religion. They do not require the student or practitioner to accept any belief or dogma. You can practice tantric meditation without adhering to the philosophy. You are not asked to accept truths without confirming that they are reasonable and acceptable to you.

Some authorities claim that Tantra started as much as 7,000 years ago. It was a systematization of various practices that had existed in India before that time. However as script had not yet been invented, we can't say exactly when it started.

We do know that Tantric knowledge passed orally from teacher to student. After the invention of script, teachers and gurus gradually started to record their knowledge, to preserve the teachings against a time when there might be few qualified teachers or students.

They also wanted to protect these teachings from misuse and abuse. So, lacking modern copyrights and passwords, they wrote their texts in a symbolic 'twilight language' whenever possible.

Tantric teachings include a comprehensive philosophy. However, the philosophy is not considered as important as the practices. As with any practical science, it's not enough to simply read about it. Practice makes perfect.

Yoga is one of the most important aspects of Tantra. People often associate yoga with Hinduism. However, yoga predates Hinduism by many centuries.

Many people who come to me think of yoga as a set of physical exercises. I may get comments or requests such as: "I don't want to learn yoga, just meditation."

This confusion is not new. There are a plethora of yoga schools today. Some just deal with physical yoga exercises. Rather than using a formal name such as 'Hatha Yoga' or 'Yoga Asanas,' they often use the simpler term 'Yoga.' But the exercises are only one part of yoga, in the same way that the black keys are only part of a piano keyboard.

The word yoga has various definitions. The broadest definition is 'union.' It describes a state where we unite our individual consciousness with the universal consciousness, which some people call God. 'Union' here can also mean that one wants to become a 'whole person'.

Yoga also means to have self-control, particularly control of the mind. Without this self-control we can make little or no spiritual progress.

Yoga has developed gradually over a long period of time. Even several thousand years ago, yogic adherents recognized certain 'limbs,' or aspects, of yoga that helped people to obtain its full benefit. About 2,000 years ago, an Indian philosopher, Patainjali, systematized these steps. His system, called *Astaunga Yoga* (the eight limbs of yoga), is a highly respected system that is still practiced today.

Patanjali published his work in one simple book, *The Yoga Aphorisms of Patanjali*. According to Swami Prabhavananda, Patanjali wrote it to 'restate yoga philosophy and practice for the person of his own period."

Although Patainjali wrote for the people of his age, he had a mature understanding of the depths and breadth of human nature. His understanding was deep enough that his book has travelled down to us today and is still regarded as a classic treatise about the practices and benefits of yoga.

Patainjali described this system as a way to clear the body and mind of the impurities that limit our spiritual vision.

These limbs, or steps, will be discussed extensively in later chapters. A brief glimpse now will help us to get an overview of Astaunga Yoga.

The first two limbs as mentioned above are Yama and Niyama. These complementary branches concern our actions and attitudes in life. Yama means 'controlled contact with others.' Niyama means 'self-regulation.' By practicing the ten steps of yama and niyama the mind is purified to the point where it is able to go deep into meditation.

The third limb, *asanas*, refers to meditation postures. It also refers to various yogic exercises that one can practice for both physical and mental health. It is essential to sit erect in meditation. This helps a person to breathe properly and to keep the mind attentive and alert. The yogic exercises tone up the glandular system. When our glands, as well as our organs, are healthy, the mind is in balance and meditation becomes easier.

*Pranayama*, the fourth limb, means 'control of the vital energy (*Prana*).' This vital energy manifests itself primarily through breathing. Thus breathing exercises can control the prana. Pranayama increases concentration and perception. It enables us to perceive subtle vibrations that the physical senses cannot perceive.

*Pratyahara*, the fifth limb, means to withdraw the attention of the mind from the physical senses. This enables the mind to concentrate deeply on the object of meditation.

*Dharana*, the sixth limb, is a technique of focusing the mind on the object of meditation. It takes the mind to a deeper level of concentration than is normally possible.

*Dhyana*, the seventh limb, means 'meditation.' In Patainjali's words, it is "an unbroken flow of thought toward the object of concentration." Although the mind is concentrated on its object, it seems to be still. If we pour oil or honey from one container to another, in a steady, unbroken stream, it may appear to be motionless. In the same way, the mind moves toward its objective while doing dhyana.

*Samadhi* is the final step or limb of Astaunga Yoga. Samadhi means 'to become one with your goal.' A serious student of yoga will have self-knowledge or complete fulfillment as their goal. Patainjali says that we attain samadhi "when, in meditation, the true nature of the object (of concentration) shines forth, undistorted by (your) mind."

## Twilight Language

Twilight Language (called *Sandhya Bhasha* in Sanskrit) is a concept that apparently originated in Tantric circles. In Twilight Language we see that words, phrases or expressions may be read in a literal, mundane, normal way and they make sense. However, one who delves deeply into the matter (this would likely be someone who is immersed or initiated into certain teachings) may see another meaning, sometimes a meaning that is the opposite of the literal, or normally accepted, meaning.

One example is a verse by an ancient Indian yogi, Tirumular,

"On the Peaked Mountain is a Summit High,
Beyond the Summit blows a Gusty Wind;
There blossomed a Flower that its fragrance spread
Within that Flower, a Bee its Nectar imbibed."

While this seems to describe a beautiful mountain setting, it is rife with twilight symbolism. The mountain in such writing often refers to a person sitting in meditation. The gusty wind likely refers to the controlled breathing of the meditator, which helps him to enter the higher realms of consciousness, suggested by the flower. Nectar, in yogic or Tantric teachings, often refers to spiritual joy.

Besides Tantric texts, the practice has been used in other traditions. It may be used to obscure the deeper meaning of a subject from those who may be curious about something but not yet able to grasp the subtlety of a subject. Or, as well, to keep the meaning from those who might misuse certain knowledge.

One example is in the Zohar, a part of the *Kabbalah*, a

book of Jewish mysticism.

One comment in the Zohar, referring to the Bible, states:

"Fools see only the garment of the Torah (the first five books of the Old Testament), the more intelligent see the body, the wise see the soul, its proper being..."

Alchemy shows another example of twilight language. On the surface alchemists seemed to be concerned with transmuting metals from one type to another. However, the more knowing alchemists were concerned with, as Titus Burckhardt calls it, 'the transmutation of the soul' to a more divine state. (As quoted in *A Sense of the Cosmos*, by Jacob Needleman.)

Perhaps the most significant misunderstanding of twilight language today is with the Tantric concept of 'maethuna'.

Maethuna refers to sexual relations. The outer meaning of maethuna is to develop self-restraint in sexuality. This one reference to sexuality in Tantra has become quite popular (and quite misinterpreted) today so that it's common to assume that Tantra is a sort of 'occult sexual science.' This is completely wrong.

The inner, twilight, meaning refers to spiritual union between the spiritual practitioner and the cosmic consciousness. In other words, this might be seen as a merger of two beings into their eternal, divine union.

Anandamurti gives an example of Twilight Language in a light vein:

"Suppose I write in twilight language "bar'a' ba'bu a'j mar gaya', bar'ii bahko pat'ha' dena'"" (a Bengali verse). Someone who does not understand its actual significance will take it to mean: "The elder brother has died today,

43

send for the elder sister-in-law (who will perform the funeral rites)." But those who understand the hint will take the correct meaning. "The elder brother (senior business partner) has gone to (the city of) Ajmer; so send the ledger (the elder sister-in-law) with the real balance sheet."

## The Evolution of Yoga

Yoga, under the strong influence of Tantra, spread throughout the Indian subcontinent. Some of the teachers made their way to China and introduced yogic practices there. Buddhism started about 2,500 years ago and accelerated the spread of yogic ideas, developing its own blend. Thus Buddhism established yogic and Tantric ideas in much of Asia, though in its early days Buddhism did not use the term 'Tantra' very much.

One reason Buddhism became popular was that Hinduism, the dominant religion of the time, had lost much of its relevance to the people. Hinduism, as with the Vedas in an earlier age, had become more ceremonial and less practical.

As teachers of Tantra started travelling outside India, Tantric ideas made inroads into local beliefs, although they did not necessarily employ the term Tantra. Taoism gained acceptance at a time when superstition and social stagnation in China were widespread. The royal court often served as a parlor for the discussion and demonstration of the arcane. Representatives of local esoteric traditions and beliefs, eager to win official favor for their own 'spiritual medicine,' came there to convince the rulers that their occult arts were the most effective. The emperors were generally eager to find a powerful brand of esotericism that might help them consolidate their power.

Cultists would describe to the royals such wonders as islands populated by immortals. They claimed to have methods of prayers that would ensure long life and health.

The teachings in one thin book of Lao-Tzu helped to free the Chinese mind from such dogmas and superstitions. Taoist yogic techniques worked to purify the body and allow the mind to "sit in forgetfulness". Writers of the time say that Lao-tzu, in meditation, could "wander freely in the origin of all beings."

Any system of social or self-development has vitality if it understands psychological and moral trends. Every great teacher or prophet understands that people want more than just bread and butter. The rational self wants logical answers and practices that touch both the heart and the mind. Anandamurti notes that the inner essences of all systems that teach about attaining permanent fulfillment are similar. It is "on account of mental differences (that) different philosophical thoughts have sprung up."

The truth of this comment may not seem so obvious on the surface, as we see that various religions and spiritual movements have texts and practices that appear quite different from each other.

However, the more I explore the differences of these various systems, the more I have to agree with Anandamurti.

Taoism and Tantra for example are two words that come from the same Sanskrit root. Both accept the unity of all existence. Both offer meditation as a way to find this unity, in the individual and the society. They both accept that nothing in the universe is static. (The Sanskrit word for the universe — *Jagat* — means 'that which moves.') They both have cosmologies that see all life evolving toward its source.

Buddhism, as it moved into China, Japan, and other Asian countries, adapted its practices somewhat to these cultures. In the early days of Buddhism in China, Chinese scholars often argued that Buddha was simply the idea of Lao-Tse transplanted into India and now being offered back to China. Buddhists refuted this claim, and its meditation seems to have taken on a Chinese, and later, Japanese, flavor. The Sanskrit word for meditation — dhyana — came to China through Buddhism. Later it was written as ch'an, the Chinese equivalent, and when these practices came to Japan it was transliterated to the Japanese word, Zen.

As Buddhism spread, it took the ideas of Tantra along with it. Buddhism, from its native soil, had picked up seeds of Tantra, eventually transplanting them to other parts of Asia.

The Middle Way of Buddhism closely relates to the Tantric 'Madhhyamika Marga', literally, the middle path. The idea is to avoid extreme attitudes or lifestyles. The Noble Eightfold Path of Buddhism is similar to the earlier conduct code of Tantra, Yama-Niyama. Later, Patanjali used the Tantric conduct code as the foundation of his Astaunga Yoga.

The goal of the spiritual practices of Buddhism and Tantra can be compared through the following quotes. The first quote is that of Buddha. The second quote is by Anandamurti, the Tantric master of the 20th century.

"We are what we think.
All that we are arises with our thoughts.
With our thoughts we make the world."

"When this individual body and mind is yours, you know all the secrets of this individual physical body and mind. And when this vast cosmos is your object, you'll know everything of this cosmos, you'll know everything of this infinite space."

Both quotes give us the responsibility of choosing how to perceive the world, and how to act upon our perceptions. They both tell us that our own perception is critical in how we see the world and act in it.

However, it seems to me that the first quote puts more emphasis on our own perception as paramount, while the second quote, that of Anandamurti, emphasizes that there is a reality outside of our own perception and we should learn how to comprehend that reality.

Buddhism later developed its own school of Tantra, known as *Vajrayana*. Vajrayana (also known as Tantrayana or Tantric Buddhism) marked the transition from speculation and theory to the practical application of Buddha's ideas. The term 'vajra' (Sanskrit for diamond, or thunderbolt) signifies the effort to find the part of the human that is indestructible. This effort is, of course, central to Tantra.

Vajrayana is generally considered to be a part of the Mahayana (Great Vehicle) school of Buddhism. One distinct feature of Vajrayana is that it claims to use practices that accelerate one's movement toward enlightenment.

Vajrayana and Tantra Yoga have many similarities. In both systems, the guru is important. They both use visualizations as aids to meditation. And both systems say that our state of mind at death is an important factor in our quest for enlightenment.

The Semitic, Middle Eastern, religions all have mystical branches that show kinship to Tantra.

Mystical Christianity, for example, refers to the direct experience of ultimate reality. The pure meditation, or dhyana, of Tantra, refers to the same experience. Some Christian mystics developed a system of 'stillness', called 'Hesychasm.' This refers to the concentration of the mind on a divine Presence. Such concentration is achieved repeating a spiritual phrase. This idea is similar to the yogic mantra. The English mystic, Mother Julian of Norwich, spoke of the mystical unity of all humanity. Protestant mysticism emphasizes that there is a divine element or 'spark' in all humans. The same ideas are found in Tantra.

Christian contemplation is sometimes called 'centering prayer' or 'silent prayer.' It is not as systematic as yogic meditation, but it does give the person a sense of quiet. Thomas Merton wrote that it is, in his experience, a "rising up out of the center of Nothingness and Silence."

Judaism has little concern with a future heaven or hell, preferring to concern itself with living a good life here and now. A similar idea in Tantra teaches that heaven and hell are within us, a result of how we have lived our lives. There are neither harps nor pits of fire in the non-material world.

The Kabbalah also talks of "the reincarnation into several successive bodies of a soul that has not attained the required perfection in a previous existence." This is of course similar to the idea of reincarnation, which is an important idea in many yogic philosophies. Some Kabbalah teachers have used yogic techniques to train their students to find inner spiritual experiences.

Sufism, the mystical branch of Islam, apparently owed its development partly to its connection with Indian mysticism. Certain branches of Sufism emphasize strict self-control and psychological insight, which are also basic to Tantra. The Egyptian Sufi, Dhu an-Nun, introduced the term 'interior knowledge.' He contrasted this to intellectual learning. This may be compared to the deeper levels of consciousness of Tantra.

Sufism also stresses the teacher/disciple relationship. In this relationship the teacher will give certain formulae for meditation and guide the student at every step of his or her development. The Sufi process includes 'dhikr' or remembrance. This involves the constant repetition of one of the names of God. This formula, like yogic mantras, expands individual consciousness.

The Semitic religions have, like the Oriental spiritual systems, an ethical base. The Ten Commandments, like the Yama-Niyama of Tantra or the Eight Noble Truths of Buddhism, are a recognized code of conduct that many people have followed for millennia.

Some type of meditation has reached into every great tradition of spiritual practice.

This brief survey suggests that humans have always had a psychic need for, in the words of an old pop song, "harmony and understanding."

In one way this psychic need is not 'sensible'; we cannot touch or smell or see it. In another way, though, it is very sensible. Tantra can help people to get the self-control and mental balance they need to find both personal and social peace. The practices we discuss in this book give you tools that you can use to help you advance from darkness to light.

Ancient Tantric masters developed a framework and guide-lines for people and society. Anandamurti has revitalized Tantra in line with the needs of present day humanity. Buddha stressed that a sense of community and adherence to human dharma (dhamma in Pali) were keys to their social and personal devel-opment. Lao-Tse gave a vision of the perfect person, the unity of all of life and the inner development of each person, which can lead to social harmony. Jesus preached a sense of service and humility.

All these teachers, and others, stressed aspects of higher consciousness that were appropriate for the people of their time and place. Although they spoke to the immediate needs of their generation, they drew their ideas and practices from the source of human experience.

In modern times Tantra has been revitalized to meet present day needs, much as Buddha and Patainjali did in the past. Insofar as these teachings have touched the core of our human nature, they will be relevant for a long time to come.

Some of the goals of Tantra concern individual development. They include cultivating the desire to do meditation as well as a deep sense of social responsibility and social service. Other aspects of social outlook in modern Tantra include such ideas as developing small, integrated communities where all the members become active partners. Another idea is the devel-opment of an attitude of human stewardship of all the world's resources (including human resources). This will replace the present attitude that we can do whatever we want with the world.

In this view, we must appreciate and respect every culture, every language, every ethnic group. We should see each one of them as if they were flowers in the garden of human civilization. A garden is beautiful not only because of the cultivation and care it receives, but because of the diversity and interplay of the different flowers.

We thus conclude our overview of Tantra. In the following chapters, we'll discuss the various aspects of Tantra in more detail.

Chapter 3

# THE PHYSICAL BODY: GATEWAY TO THE MIND AND SOUL

The greatest discovery of my generation is that a human being
can alter his life by altering his attitudes of mind.
— William James (psychologist)

The concept of total wellness recognizes that our every thought,
word, and behavior affects our greater health and well-being.
And we, in turn, are affected not only emotionally but also
physically and spiritually.
— Greg Anderson (1964 - ____) US basketball player

If you ask someone, "How's your health?" you'll most likely get
a response about the state of the person's physical body.

If you ask a more general question, such as, "How are you
doing?" you may hear about both their physical health and how
they are feeling emotionally.

A still more general question, such as, "What's new with
you?" may get a response that covers a bit more about the
person. The person then may go beyond health issues and talk
about their work or studies, or relationships or ambitions.

However, few people will answer such questions by giving
you much idea of their spiritual quests, insights or visions.

As noted in chapter one, there is an unbreakable link among
the three levels of our self. The part of us we call the body, which
is the physical body, is the most obvious and the most tangible.

But is it any more 'real' than the mind or soul?

The life and work of Dr. Patch Adams, a medical doctor who
is also a social activist, citizen diplomat, professional clown,
performer, and author, illustrates the point that though a doctor

51

deals with healing the physical body, the body is connected to a greater whole. Dr. Adams' healing shows the human, physical body as part of a greater self. So his healing tends to include methods that are not just medical. He also uses, humor, personal and social engagement and the ideas and practice of eco-community.

Such a concept of healing goes along with what I observe: though standard medical healing is necessary sometimes, it is often true that the sickness – or health – of the physical body is just a reflection of the level of health or well being of the whole person, and perhaps of the society.

An example of the body-mind relation is that we feel pain and pleasure through our body, but our mind decides how we should respond to those feelings. Our numerous nerves (on the skin, the tongue, ears, nose, etc.) send signals to the brain. The brain decides which of these signals are pleasant and which are painful. Under normal circumstances we have some freedom to adjust the 'pleasure/pain' dial. I turn the air conditioner higher or lower because my brain 'reads' certain signals from my skin as either cold or hot. I stop eating because my stomach tells me I am full.

The brain may interpret a signal it receives as giving either long-term benefit or short term benefit. Our socialization also plays an important role in how our brain deals with the signals it receives. Immediate pleasure or pain is another factor. Cigarettes exemplify both these points. Even if I know cigarettes are bad for my health, I may ignore this knowledge if I get enough pleasure out of smoking. For most people, the harshness of tobacco may be an initial put-off, but the desire to be accepted by their peer group may make a person continue to smoke; eventually it becomes pleasurable. So the rational mind may tell us that smoking is bad, but this message may be overridden by our desire for instant gratification.

On the other end of the pleasure-pain spectrum, I may

THE PHYSICAL BODY: GATEWAY TO THE MIND AND SOUL

struggle to complete a hard physical workout, knowing there are benefits for my body and my overall strength, even if, at the moment, my body is suffering.

Sometimes the brain may altogether misinterpret a signal. In my university days I had the habit of going barefoot, even for months at a time. Once I was waiting in a line, and chatting with a friend as we slowly moved forward. After a while I felt an odd sensation rush up my leg, something I'd never felt before. I thought something like, "That's curious. What is that feeling?" I looked down and saw that I'd stepped on a lit cigarette that someone had discarded. Then I felt pain!

The senses and motor organs are like the mind's window to the world. If the physical body is healthy and the 'psychic body' is calm, they can communicate well with each other. The effectiveness of the communication is determined by the health of our organs, nerves and brain.

Meditation fine-tunes the mind. However, if we neglect our physical health and needs, the mind cannot easily enjoy the benefits that meditation offers. It will be very preoccupied with the discomforts and troubles of the body. So the body also needs love and care.

Yogic masters have developed many practices and exercises to create a balanced connection between the body, mind and spirit. They know a healthy body is very important for the development of the mind and spirit. Yoga asanas, vegetarianism and fasting are some of the most popular of these practices. Anandamurti, the modern Tantra master, has added a few more practices to the list and revived some that have fallen into disuse. We will discuss these practices later in this chapter.

**Seven Tips for Health**

The purpose of the entire creation is to get and give happiness. Ideally, there is no scope for any disease, pain and suffering, unless we disobey the laws of nature or ignore the body's signs of distress. The fundamental law, on which this physical and mental health depends, is a loving friendship between our self, our habits and our body.

Today's society is based on exploitation and abuse. There is no harmony amongst people, nor within the individual, or with the environment. Rather than deeply blissful, human life is often hardship, which we endure. What we call 'healthy' in no way reflects the potential of vitality, joy and gratitude that nature offers us.

The fundamental task in recovering this sublime health and restoring the natural balance within is to build a relation of compassion with each and everything, especially with those factors that rekindle the life forces and which we should consider our real friends.

First among these is our Supreme Friend, the universal Cosmic Entity, on whom the existence of the entire universe and everything within it depends. In our quest for health we can list seven factors as our foremost friends.

1. *The Power of the Cosmic Entity*: The movement of the entire universe is based upon one single force. The power which makes the planets, stars and galaxies move in their respective orbits is the same power that exists within a small cell and directs its varied functions. This is the Cosmic Entity, our Supreme Friend, and harmony with this force is the principal source of sentient health and infinite happiness.

2. *The Power of Positive Mind:* The ability and speed of the human mind are unparalleled. Even the latest computers cannot match the agility, power and creativity of the mind.

   But this incredible mental force can work in two directions—positive and negative. The moment we have a positive state of mind, all the cells and their biochemical processes in the body also function more positively.

   The treatment methods we use for our health and happiness may work in absence of a positive mind, but the result will be limited. In the absence of a positive mind, life will be full of misery and pain. On the other hand, a positive mind can bring about health and well-being beyond imagination.

3. *Fresh Air:* Our friend every second of the day, air has to be with us always. If for a few minutes we would be cut off from fresh air, nothing can save our existence. Just as we learn how to eat by studying nutrition, we must come to understand the proper use of fresh air to clean our body, make our mind peaceful, and revitalize our whole system.

4. *Sunlight:* The rhythm of the sun is the discipline of our whole existence. If its temperature will start to drop, existence on this earth will be deeply affected. Our body temperature is regulated every day by the sun's energy. The sun is the source of all our energy and can cure any imbalance of the body. For thousands of years, the sun's temperature was the only hope for humans to survive the tremendous cold. The sun is the source for the life-giving rains, the greening of the earth, the growing of our food, the strength of our health.

5. *Water:* Water is the friend of every hour, whom we need in many different ways in our body to enrich our own health and environment.

6. *Relaxation:* This is the only time when our body and mind get time to restore themselves. Though we have the physical strength, we can not work continuously because the body requires periodic rest to cleanse itself. When we relax our body, it starts to recharge and the mind recovers its strength. Rest lets nature supply us with energy and work through us. Thus relaxation is very important in maintaining our natural strength.

7. *Positive food habits:* Most diseases are caused by eating the wrong foods in the wrong amount and at the wrong time. Controlling the quality, amount and timing of the food we use, it becomes friendly to our all round health and the source of our mental peace. At the time of sickness or discomfort, positive food habits can cure and restore our strength.

— By Ac. Jyotiishvarananda

## The Links between Our Bodies

We can see the link between the body and mind in our daily activities. A toothache or headache, for example, can cloud our thinking and judgment. Taking the wrong food or drink may significantly affect our minds. Watch a child, when he eats too much sugar and the negative effects may be very obvious.

Once I'd gone out for the day with the 6-year old son of a friend of mine. We visited various museums and parks. Later in the afternoon we passed an ice cream shop and I went against my intuition and asked him if he wanted some ice cream. Almost immediately after eating his cone he started crying and whining and could not be placated. This can of course happen with adults too, though we may disguise our bad mood more than a child will.

Our body-mind link plays out every day in numerous ways. Too much food will make you sluggish at best. Sit in a room with no air circulation and soon you are becoming drowsy. You also may have trouble thinking clearly when you are breathing very hard after strong physical exercise. At that moment, if you try to think about your schedule for the day or who you last talked to on the phone you may not remember the answer so easily. Your brain cannot think clearly because you are lacking oxygen. Deep thinking, on the other hand, usually accompanies deep, slow breathing. Thus our physical state has a lot to do with the effectiveness of our mind. Few people can think as clearly when they are ill as they can when they are healthy.

While the mind-body link is clear, the link between the physical and spiritual bodies may not be as obvious. It is also not so direct, since the mind links the two. The mind and body together determine how we respond or react in many situations. It thus follows that if physical illness limits our mental effectiveness, it also limits our spiritual awareness.

As well, what one believes about herself can affect you whether it is actually true or not. In his book, "Love, Medicine and Miracles" Bernie Siegel tells of two men in a hospital who were given each other's diagnosis. One man, who had cancer, was mistakenly told that he was okay. He left the hospital in good health. The other man had a minor problem, but was told he had cancer. He passed away in the hospital.

So, for optimum health we need to work with both the body and the mind. From a spiritual perspective this is important also, since it's hard, when we are sick, to reach an optimum spiritual state.

Several yogic practices are quite good at keeping the body/mind connection open and flowing. They include *half-bath*, fasting and certain yogic dances. There are also many more;

some of them may be just right for you. If your body has always been like an old pick-up truck, try some of these practices. After a while your friends will think you traded it in for a Porsche.

All these practices can be very useful at the right time. A qualified meditation teacher can give you personal instruction regarding the practices you learn from this book.

In chapter one, we discussed the need for discipline in our lives. It provides us with a structure or foundation which helps our self-development. The purpose of yogic discipline is to give us control over our physical and mental bodies so we can develop our spiritual self.

Self-control, or discipline, is most important if we want mental control. The amount of mental control we have, the amount of inner strength we have, makes a lot of difference in how we manifest the strength of our convictions.

A famous yogic story tells how a mother went to a highly respected guru and asked him to tell her son to stop eating too much sugar. The guru told the mother to come back in a few days and he would then tell her son. When they returned, he firmly told the boy not to eat too much sugar.

The mother thanked him but also asked the guru why she had to come back. Why could he not tell her son the first time? The guru said that at that time he himself was still eating too much sugar, so his words would not have been effective or convincing.

Many of our personal problems relate to lack of self-control. Some common problems include smoking, over-eating and alcoholism. There are other problems which are not as obvious or important, but which also reduce our effectiveness or happiness in life. Some of these problems include talking too much, procrastination and shyness. There are many more.

If you want to get rid of these habits, it may not be enough to just say: "I'm going to stop drinking (or smoking or over-eating, etc)."

For one thing, the mind and body always want to be kept

busy. If you stop one type of behavior, you must replace it with something else. The physical disciplines discussed in this chapter are an important key to help you attain maximum benefit from the mental and spiritual disciplines.

It's also true hat the way we approach our self-improvement is important. Sometimes it seems to me the mind doesn't hear the word 'no'. That is, if you say to yourself: "I will not overeat," or "I will not smoke cigarettes" the mind seems to forget that you told it to 'not' do something. One may argue that this type of phrasing is reminding you of the habit you want to break.

So, while it is important to determine and decide what behavior you want to change, don't spend too much energy reminding yourself of what you want to get away from. Rather, look toward the result you want. In the case of a smoker, the result he wants should not be stated as, "In (one month) I will not be smoking." Of course he needs to realize that he wants to quit smoking. But it may be helpful to envision the positive state of his health after he has stopped smoking. Thus he can try to see what he will be doing (for example, more sports, being more sociable, etc) and the optimum health that he knows he can have, rather than on what he doesn't want.

Meditation of course can help one to develop and hold onto this positive attitude, since meditation practices are designed to remind us of our positive potential.

While meditation is the key to the development of the whole self, the physical practices outlined in this chapter are very important aids to meditation. These practices are discussed below.

*Cleanliness*:
It is difficult to do meditation when you are dirty, sweaty, hot or tired. Cleanliness both improves our health and helps us in our meditation.

Dirt comes to us not only from outside, but also from inside.

We discharge large amounts of waste through defecation and urination.

We also discharge waste through sweat.

So, a daily bath is therefore highly recommended to clean the skin, the largest organ in our body. I bathe when I wake up in the morning and I can then start my day fresh and revitalized.

A note about traditional yogic bathing techniques. Cool water is recommended for bathing whenever possible. Too much hot water may dull the nerves. You may find it difficult, though, to take a cold or cool bath. As an alternative, start with cool water, continue with warm water and finish the bath with a little cool water. Sitting or squatting is a good way to bathe. It is most useful for men, as it prevents any undue pressure on the genitals.

Upon first contact cool water can shock the system. In order to minimize the shock, the yogic method is to first pour water on the navel and genitals, then on the lower back opposite the navel.

After that, water is poured over the top of the head, so that it trickles down the spine. Then wash the rest of your body. Swimmers and divers do something similar. They walk into the water feet first, then legs, waist and then the whole body. In this way, they give themselves time to adjust to the cool water.

As it's not always easy to take a full bath every time we are

feeling dirty or tired and need invigoration, a process called *half-bath* provides a good alternative. It only takes a minute or less to do it and has many of the benefits of a complete bath.

The accompanying diagram shows how to do half-bath step by step. First, pour cool water over the genital area, below the navel. Then pour water from the knees down to the feet. Do the same from the elbows to the fingers. Next, fill the mouth with water and splash water in the open eyes twelve times (or more if you prefer). Spit the water out of the mouth. Then tilt the head back and pour water into the nostrils three times. Let it drain into the back of the throat each time and spit it out. Then you can clean your throat by using

your right middle finger, gargling and spitting out whatever phlegm might be there. Finish the half bath by washing behind the ears and the back of the neck with cool water.

Let's see why we do half bath. We have five motor organs: the

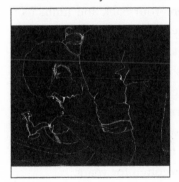

hands, feet, vocal cord, genitals and anus. We also have five sensory organs: the eyes, ears, nose, tongue and skin. As the day goes on, they become tired, heated and dirty. These ten organs are the connection between the mind and the world. When they are exhausted, so is our mind. Clean and cool them and you

calm and refresh your mind.

Splashing water in the open eyes and cooling the extremities slows the heart rate and increases blood flow to the heart and brain. Scientists call this the 'diving reflex.' When mammals dive under water, the act of diving causes their metabolism to slow down so they can stay under water longer. For us the slower metabolism signifies relaxation. Splashing water also cleans dirt out of the eyes and reduces eyestrain. One friend of mine started wearing glasses in his early teens. In his twenties, soon after learning meditation, he started doing half-bath. He soon found his eyesight was improving. Within a year he was able to give up his glasses. More than 20 years later, he still doesn't need them. He attributes that to the regular practice of half-bath, particularly the practice of splashing water in his eyes.

When we clean the nasal passages with water, it helps prevent colds. Cleaning the nasal passages of course also improves our breathing. Cleaning the throat, as noted, clears out mucus and phlegm.

Communities that live in hot, desert climates also have a style similar to half-bath, to keep themselves refreshed or cool. And Muslims, particularly those living in hot climates, often do a similar practice before entering the mosque for prayer.

*Exercises and movement:*
Imagine you are sitting on soft grass, on the side of a hill. A gentle breeze cools you in the afternoon sun. Your back and limbs feel limber and flexible. You close your eyes and soon dive deep into meditation. Solitude, peace and quiet dance through your mind. Alone and still, your inner eye glides through the many facets of your personality. It spots various rough edges of your nature and tries to understand their origins and reasons for still being part of you. Perhaps happiness and a sort of sweet agony mix as you stroll through your self and unveil to your conscious mind so much that has remained hidden or forgotten for years.

At the end of your meditation stand up, stretch and return to the world. You slowly return to the city and the daily grind. The stillness and peace you found in meditation doesn't have to disappear in the vapor of memories. As you go to shop, study, work and meet your friends, you can also maintain a still, quiet center in your heart and mind.

While yogic meditation is one important tool to help us maintain this peace and stillness, yogic movement exercises are also very beneficial.

Yogic exercises are called *asanas*.

'Asana' means a position which is easily held. Asanas are exercises, but they have little to do with building muscles. They do build a stronger nervous system. They also help to balance the secretions of our endocrine glands (which include the pancreas, gonads, thyroid, parathyroid, adrenal, pituitary and pineal glands). When these glands are functioning well, they help our emotions to be more balanced. They also improve the function of the various organs.

Certain asanas, for example, can help a fearful person to overcome his fear. They can help a shy person to get rid of his shyness and a nervous person to be calmer and collected. Many physical problems, such as those of the stomach, lungs and back, can be cured through asanas.

While medical care is certainly important at the right time, as noted elsewhere in this book, the body has a great ability to heal itself if given time, rest and good nutrition. Asanas assist this process. They are something you can do, in a very natural, un-mechanical way. "Yoga," Swami Vishnudevananda says, "aims to remove the root cause of all diseases, not to treat its symptoms."

In ancient times, many yogis lived in nature, in the forests and jungles. They invented some asanas by observing the animals around them. They would notice that a certain animal had a specific trait. They concluded that if they practiced the posture of that animal they might acquire something of the animal's nature. We associate specific qualities, such as powerful memory, strong digestion, fearlessness etc. with particular animals.

Of course, it must have soon become apparent that the effect of a posture on any animal was probably due to the fact that the animal was spending a large amount of time in this position every day and thus its organs, glands, nervous system were being 'conditioned' by the position. So, the yogis realized the need for regular practice of a position to acquire its benefits.

For example, a peacock has very strong digestion. So the

yogis developed a position, which is similar to a peacock's posture. This position puts acute pressure on the stomach. People found they could improve their digestion if they practiced this position.

Gradually the yogis realized that not only physical changes resulted from the practice of the asanas. Certain mental traits also developed with the regular practice of asanas. They found, for example, that an asana called 'viirasana'(brave posture) helped people to become more courageous. Another posture, 'kurmakasana'(tortoise posture), helps a person to become more introverted. Through many generations of experiment and practice, yogis developed a body of knowledge related to the effects of asanas. As modern medical researchers explore yogic practice more, I believe they will be able to confirm the theories and experiences of the yogis.

It is said that there are perhaps 50,000 asanas. However, Anandamurti has compiled a list of about 50 asanas plus some related postures, which are most useful. A judicious combination of these asanas can help one to keep good health. Usually a student will practice three to five asanas in the morning and a similar number at night to get the most benefit from the asanas.

As with meditation or anything else you want to learn, practice makes perfect in the field of asanas. The accompanying diagrams show a few of the main asanas.

Here are some helpful hints for getting the most benefit from the regular practice of asanas.

- Use a blanket or mat and don't do asanas in the open air or in a drafty room as this can lead to a cold or to stiff joints.
- Wear loose clothing, or, if alone, just underwear. Underwear should be supportive, not loose.
- Asanas should be done on an empty stomach, so wait at least 2-1/2 to 3 hours after eating, before doing them.
- After finishing your set of asanas, massage your body, paying

 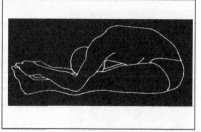

particular attention to the joints. Yogic postures stimulate secretions from various glands which are useful to the body. A massage will enable the secretions to be reabsorbed into the skin, thus adding to the health and luster of the skin.

- After completing the massage, lie down on your back, close your eyes and relax. Keep your arms on the floor, by your side. This posture is called 'Shavasana' (corpse pose). It is very helpful in creating a deep sense of relaxation. Stay in this position for two minutes or longer. If you feel a lot of tension during the day, do this posture whenever you can. It can relieve much mental and physical strain.

Although yoga asanas are popular in many parts of the world, yoga also includes some lesser-known movement therapies that are also highly beneficial. Two of these are dances which have great physical and mental benefits.

One is called *Kaoshikii*. It was invented by Anandamurti in 1978. He describes it as a dance exercise and a medicine: "It is a sort of panacea for almost all female diseases, and for many male diseases of younger boys... (and) for most liver diseases. It assures safe deliveries for ladies and also checks the advent of old age."

Although the dance benefits mainly women, some of its qualities are useful for everyone. For example, it makes the spine flexible, it exercises all the glands and limbs and helps to cure some types of arthritis.

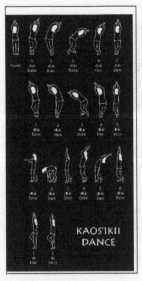

KAOS'IKII
DANCE

The diagram herein shows how to do it. You should learn the fine points and the rhythm of the dance from a teacher. Each step or position has a different symbolic meaning. The word 'Kaoshikii' refers to the primordial force of creation or the energy in the universe. The dance develops mental stamina and strength. However, the spiritual meaning is also important. I can summarize this by noting the ideation of the last two steps which signify the overcoming of all obstacles and one's establishment in the cosmic rhythm.

Another beneficial dance is *Tandava*. Tandava was performed by males from ancient times in India. The word 'Tandava' derives from the root 'tandu', which means 'jumping.' Jumping is a dominant feature of this dance. The heavy pounding movements and some of the leg positions can negatively affect a woman's hormonal balance. This dance stimulates the male hormones, thus making it unsuitable for women.

As with Kaoshikii, Tandava has a practical and symbolic meaning and confers physical, mental and spiritual benefits. It is an exercise for the brain. It helps cure low blood sugar when combined with proper asanas and diet. It increases courage and will power, as well as the memory. Symbolically it is a fight between good and evil or life and death.

Ideally the dancer will hold either a knife or torch in his right hand to symbolize life (or a force that conquers death and darkness) and either a skull or snake in his left hand. symbolizing death. Thus symbolically he is jumping between life and death in an effort to conquer the forces of darkness within and without himself, using the forces of light and life.

At the start of tandava, the dancer will hold his arms straight out. He then jumps straight up as far as he can. At the moment he starts to jump he also bends his knees so they will touch against his chest in mid-air. After his feet come to touch the ground, he straightens up.

Here are some other tips for keeping or improving your health. Regular exercise is important. No matter how many yogic exercises you do, you still need other physical outlets. You may like walking. Anandamurti gives a hint for walkers. He says to walk until you sweat. However one must adjust this advice to their own place. In cold or very dry climates, this may not be realistic as one may need to do an excessive amount of walking to sweat. In a very humid climate you may sweat just walking out of your front door. Wherever you live, though, take a good walk as often as possible.

Running, swimming, bicycling or other sports are all very useful for developing physical vigor. Don't think that if you are 'getting a bit old' you will not benefit from exercise. Deepak Chopra stresses that at any age it is important to maintain and even improve our health and physical strength.

Eating is a science in itself, or at least an art. I've come across so much advice about proper eating that I finally realized they cannot all be applied at one time. Keeping this in mind, consider the following points and adapt the ones that seem suitable to you:

- Don't eat more than four times a day
- Make breakfast or lunch your main meal, not dinner
- Try to finish eating at least two hours before sleeping
- Eat raw food (vegetables and fruits) regularly
- Chew your food well
- "Food taken in anger turns to poison," is an old yogic saying. So eat when your mind and surroundings are calm
- Wait some time (1/2 hour to 1-1/2 hours) after eating before drinking

- Wait several hours between meals to allow for digestion
- Rest after lunch, walk after dinner
- A yogic formula for eating a meal is to half fill your stomach with food, 1/4 fill it with water and leave 1/4 empty. This may be hard to measure, of course, but I suggest that you stop eating before you are full.
- Some of Anandamurti's secrets for a long, healthy life include:

  • Undertake some physical labor regularly
  • Eat as soon as you feel hungry
  • Go to sleep as soon as you feel sleepy
  • Practice meditation regularly
  • Fast periodically
  • Do half-bath before meditation, meals and sleep
  • Eat yogurt and raw foods regularly
  • Rise early in the morning; don't oversleep
  • Drink sufficient water, small quantities at a time. Adding lemon and a little salt is beneficial

Pure, fresh air has the power to cure diseases. Take deep, full breaths when you are outside in the clean air.

These suggestions can be very beneficial, but you should decide which of them are appropriate for you now. Our bodies, minds and daily life change, so we may need to adjust our diet and exercise routines also.

*Water*

Water is very important for keeping our overall health. We've discussed bathing and half-bath and we've mentioned drinking. I want to expand on this a bit.

Since water is essential for the maintenance of life, it is important to drink enough water daily. I just mentioned drinking 'small quantities at a time.' This varies from person to person, but a cup at a time may be average. In hot climates, where it is essential to drink as much as is reasonably possible, three or four liters a day is not too much. In moderate and cool climates we should still drink at least two liters per day. This helps to flush all the waste out of our system. It also purifies our blood. Liquids other than water can also be beneficial. Drinks that are healthy for both the body and mind are preferable.

The use of water after urination is also beneficial. When we urinate some residual urine may be left in the bladder and in the genitals. If we pour some water over the genitals after urination this will clean and cool the genitals and help to eject the last traces of urine from the bladder. Certain genital and bladder diseases, such as hydrocele, can be prevented by this practice. The cooling effect of pouring cool water also helps prevent the over-stimulation of the genital organs.

Yogic practices are very detailed and even include guidelines relating to our underwear. Proper underwear can help us keep our sexual thoughts in balance and also protect the genital organs.

For men the recommended underwear is a *lungota*. It is more supportive than the underwear most men wear these days. Any male teacher in Ananda Marga can explain how to wear it. For women a bra and panties are recommended.

---

**Dynamic Health**

It is very, very important, I think, that you go to healthy eating in order to obtain from it whatever you need, in order to live at a higher level of well-being, with greater awareness, and to go beyond it. For what being healthy is really about is never having to think about health. I believe the goals of healthy eating, doing yoga, taking up a fitness course, meditation, deep relaxation and stress control should be to bring each one of us to the point where we no

---

longer have to concern ourselves with being healthy.

Then health becomes what it is meant to be, a foundation, not an end in itself. The last thing in the world that I would ever ask anyone to do is to spend all their time thinking about how they should eat or what they should do to stay healthy. Sometimes people come up to me and say "I could never do all the things in your books." I say "I don't expect you to. Go to a book. Find what works you in it. Use it. Then forget the rest."

Each one of us is totally individual, and the details of our diet and of the exercise that we need are individual too. So you need to find what works for you, make use of it, and then let go of it once it has done its job, and move on. For what food is about, what health is about fundamentally is to establish a relationship for each one of us with life, where we are in a state of balance. That does not mean a static state; but immersed in a dynamic living process, in which we are able to relate with the whole of our being to the world in which we live.

Good eating is probably one of the most important requirements for good health, a way of helping to bring us to the center of our own being, so that we are able to live at ease with our body and to experience different levels of reality in all their splendor. But nourishment doesn't just come through vitamins, minerals, proteins and fatty acids, and you cannot think of food only in biochemical terms.

When you look at food, you are looking at a whole energetic system. The food that we eat comes from our environment, it links us up with our environment, it gives us information. Some of the information is biochemical, in terms of vitamins, minerals, and so forth; some of it is energetic. It is the great volume of top quality information

implicit in a diet high in raw foods which makes it so effective at rebalancing the body, so that you begin to experience your own being and your own center and your sense of natural joy. For joy is natural to the human being; it is not something we have to create. It is there already! All we have to do is clear away whatever is in the way of our experiencing it.
— By Leslie Kenton (from www.ru.org)

## Vegetarianism

"I don't eat junk foods and I don't think junk thoughts."
— Peace Pilgrim

"It may indeed be doubted whether butchers' meat is anywhere a necessary of life. Grain and other vegetables... afford the most plentiful, the most wholesome, the most nourishing, and the most invigorating diet. Decency nowhere requires that any man should eat butchers' meat."
— Economist Adam Smith in "The Wealth of Nations"

"In all the round world of Utopia there is no meat. There used to be. But now we cannot stand the thought of slaughter-houses. And, in a population that is all educated, and at about the same level of physical refinement, it is practically impossible to find anyone who will hew a dead ox or pig. I can still remember as a boy the rejoicings over the closing of the last slaughterhouse."
— H. G. Wells, vision of the future in "A Modern Utopia"

Food is of course meant to give us physical nutrition. Most foods also affect our mind to some degree.

For the sake of this discussion, we can classify food as either vegetarian or non-vegetarian. However, there is another method of classification. This system divides food, as well as all other aspects of life, into three categories. As you might guess, not all vegetarian foods have equal benefit for everyone. We choose our food according to our nature, and according to our lifestyle.

Acharya Shraddhananda, a noted yoga teacher from India, writes: "The types of food which a creature eats varies in proportion to its degree of evolution. While lowly developed insects and fish and animals can easily digest garbage or rotten flesh, more evolved species require more subtle foods for their superior minds. Humans... require more subtle food than the higher animals do."

These three categories of food are termed sentient, mutative and static. A person of sentient – or conscious – nature is 'finely sensitive in perception and feeling; aware.' Humans are more sentient than other creatures, though of course some people are more sentient than others. Meditation helps to increase our awareness, our consciousness, and food can either support our efforts in this direction, or work against it. A food that helps us maintain or increase our awareness is called a sentient food.

Someone or something mutative is 'prone to change; inconstant.' It indicates a restless nature.

Those of static nature are 'characterized by a lack of movement, animation or progression; showing little change.'

Sentient foods are healthy for the body and help to sharpen and clear the mind. Mutative foods stimulate the body and mind. They may be good for the body, but also tend to make the mind restless. Static foods tend to make the mind dull. Some of them may be good for the body but they are generally not good for the mind.

These categories of food were first observed thousands of years ago. Much experiment and experience has confirmed the validity of these classifications. Of course, as time, place and person vary, there can be some variation in these classifications.

If you live in a very cold climate, you may need to eat some mutative foods, even if you prefer only sentient foods. The mutative foods can give you more body heat and physical energy. Also, at times of sickness certain foods or medicines which are mutative may be necessary, regardless of your food preferences. And finally, no matter how strict you are in your food habits, it is better to eat any of the three types of food than to starve to death.

Some of the sentient foods include: fruits and nuts, most vegetables, most legumes and grains, dairy foods and most herbs and spices.

Mutative foods include caffeinated and carbonated drinks (coffee, tea, soft drinks) and many medicines. As well, overeating or overdrinking can make sentient food have a mutative or static effect on the body and mind.

Static foods include meat, poultry, eggs, fish, onions, garlic, mushrooms, alcohol, tobacco and intoxicants, and stale food.

Our mental state, our 'personality,' will often guide us to the type of foods we need. I have found that this process is sometimes faulty. Our food habits developed in our youth and if our lifestyle changes significantly, we may not easily change our food habits. If we want to adopt, however, a new style of eating, we may need information from books or experienced people to navigate us through our nutritional changes.

Many people who take up meditation develop the desire to purify their diet. Meditation makes the mind more sensitive than it used to be. This sensitivity extends to many aspects of life, including diet. A sentient diet is most helpful in balancing and controlling the mind.

Some vegetarian foods such as onions, garlic and mushrooms are considered static in nature. These foods are quite popular among vegetarians. Garlic has some health benefits, though garlic as well as onions, unsettle the mind. They excite the tongue, and stimulate appetite and digestion. If you practice regular meditation and eat these foods, however, you may find it difficult to concentrate. Mushrooms are a fungus. They grow on dead matter and carry this vibration into you. They make the mind dull and, as we know, some mushrooms are poisonous.

Researcher Dr. Robert Beck notes that garlic is a poison. He has written in the March 1996 issue of *Nexus* magazine: "If you have any patients who have low-grade headaches or attention deficit disorder, they can't quite focus on the computer in the afternoon, just do an experiment... Take these people off garlic and see how much better they get, very very shortly."

Emphasizing the poisonous affects of garlic, he said in the above quoted lecture: "Any of you who are organic gardeners know that if you don't want to use DDT, garlic will kill anything in the way of insects."

Vegetarians are not people who eat just vegetables. True, some people think the word 'vegetarian' is derived from the word 'vegetable,' which includes fruits, grains, nuts, seeds, as well as vegetables. Others, however, argue that the word takes its origin from the Latin, 'vegetus', which means 'active or vigorous.'

This indicates that vegetarian food gives life and carnivorous food is static or lifeless.

When an animal is being killed, it feels terror and great pain. This is passed on to the eater in the form of hormones and toxic by-products which have passed through its bloodstream and into the flesh we later eat. The Nutrition Institute of America notes: "The flesh of an animal carcass is loaded with toxic blood and other waste by-products."

I have noticed that most of the meat we consume is bought in a very processed, packaged form. To me this suggests that we don't really want to be reminded about where the meat originally comes from.

So, two broad reasons emerge why a vegetarian diet is a more suitable for human beings than is a meat diet. One reason is physiological. Our organism, from our mouth down to our intestines, is vegetarian. Dr. John Christopher, a well-respected natural healer in the USA, gives a graphic example of this. He suggests that we set the bodies of a gorilla and a human next to each other. If we cut them open, we would see that their bodies appear very similar. Both have very long digestive tracts, about ten to twelve times the length of the body. Both have similar digestive juices. We find these two features in all the vegetarian species of the animal kingdom. Fruits, vegetables, grains, etc., digest and pass through the body at a slow pace. So a long digestive tract enables the body to 'pick and choose' what of the food it wants. Carnivores have short digestive tracts as flesh rots rapidly and therefore must be digested more quickly.

According to Dr. Christopher, the main physical difference between the vegetarian gorilla and the (sometimes vegetarian) human is that the gorilla is a lot stronger and healthier than the human.

Of course when humans eat meat it's quite different from when animals do. We cook it and flavor it in various ways. Culinary scientists put much of their effort into finding palatable, tasty ways for humans to take their meat.

The second reason vegetarianism is more appropriate concerns harmony, morality, ethics. It also has to do with economics. A word on economics later. The city of Rishikesh, in eastern India, exemplifies the relationship between inner harmony and vegetarianism. It is a city noted for the many yogis who travel through and live there. There are an immense amount of yoga centers there. Spirituality seems to pervade the atmosphere more than in other places. And in Rishikesh all the restaurants are vegetarian.

In Occidental history, we know that Pythagoras, the great mathematician, recommended a vegetarian diet to remind us of the kinship of all animals. Vegetarianism, he noted, represented human benevolence to all creatures. Later philosophers, such as Plato, Plutarch and Epicurus favored a vegetarian diet as a statement against the bloody sacrifices of the day. They also associated vegetarianism with a belief in reincarnation. More importantly, it corresponded with their search for principles of cosmic harmony.

Pythagoras noted that: "For as long as men massacre animals, they will kill each other. Indeed, he who sows the seed of murder and pain cannot reap joy and love."

The ethical foundation of yoga also supports vegetarianism. Ethics will be discussed in detail in chapter four. Here suffice it to say that ethics are guidelines to help the mind attain a state where negative tendencies do not affect it. The first point in this code of ethics is the practice of non-injury to others. If we seriously wish to practice non-injury it follows that we should eat food that involves the least possible harm to living beings. Thus we should eat food that is less conscious, less developed. Fruits, vegetables, grains, etc., fit this criterion.

By the time the great Greek civilization emerged, meat eating had become common among humans. According to the book *What's Wrong With Eating Meat?* our early ancestors were vegetarian, as nature ordained us to be. However, during the last Ice Age, when their traditional diet was unavailable, humans started eating animals out of necessity. Some groups, such as the Inuits who live in very cold climates, continued this custom, out of necessity, while others continued out of habit or conditioning and a desire for the taste.

Vegetarianism is of course often associated with sensitivity to the suffering of animals. This sensitivity was a cornerstone of the modern vegetarian movement in Europe and America, in the 17th and 18th centuries. Some Protestant groups, taking the Bible literally, became vegetarian. Voltaire, Shelley and Thoreau were all vegetarians, not only for health, but also for their moral satisfaction. In this era, "vegetarianism tended to be combined with other efforts toward a humane and a cosmically harmonious way of life."

In modern times, ethics has been a prime motivation for vegetarians. In recent times Leo Tolstoy, George Bernard Shaw and Albert Einstein are among the most famous vegetarians.

Athletes have also noticed the vitality of a vegetarian diet. The record of success of vegetarian athletes is imposing. In many experiments and endurance tests, vegetarians have demonstrated up to twice the stamina of meat eaters. Tests were based on how long a person could walk or run, and how fast they recover after the exercise. It was found that in endurance, strength and rate of recovery vegetarians generally outdo meat eaters.

These are some of the reasons top athletes take up vegetarianism. Some great swimmers, such as Murray Rose, a triple gold-medal winner in the Olympics, and Johnny Weissmuller, were vegetarian. Paavo Nurmi, the Finnish runner, one of the most accomplished athletes of his era, was vegetarian. More recently, Carl Lewis and the basketball player Bill Walton as well as Dave Scott, who has won the world triathlon ("iron man") championship six times, are dedicated vegetarians.

Many distance athletes, such as cyclists, runners and swimmers, avoid meat, which they find too heavy and which takes too much time to digest. In 1996 *Time* magazine polled many Olympic athletes to select the ten greatest athletes in the 100-year history of the modern Olympics. Nurmi and Lewis were selected numbers one and two respectively.

Vegetarianism offers benefits to almost everyone on this planet. Scientists associate many types of cancer with a regular meat diet. Smoking and drinking are also linked with many diseases. Several friends have told me that a vegetarian diet, combined with meditation, makes it easy to give up smoking and drinking. One Chinese herbal doctor told me that oriental medical theories classify meat as a very yang, or concentrated, salty food. Tobacco and alcohol are very yin, or expansive. So one who eats a lot of meat may tend to use tobacco and alcohol to balance the effect of meat.

Meat comes to us laden with many toxins. Many poisonous chemicals that come from fertilizers and pesticides are deposited in concentrated form in the flesh of the animals that eat the plants and grasses. Such chemicals are also found in the vegetables, fruits and grains we eat, but as we are taking the vegetables from much lower down the food chain, the concentration of chemicals is much lower. Meat, for example, contains 13 times as much DDT as vegetarian foods exposed to the same chemicals. Animals raised for human consumption are also treated with cancer-causing chemicals (for growth, color, etc.) that make their way into us.

Besides cancer, vegetarianism can keep us from other diseases. *The Journal of the American Medical Association* reports: "A vegetarian diet can prevent 90-97% of heart diseases."

The information I've just noted is of course for individual consideration. In a sense, though, the question is also economic and social. Many countries spend a huge amount of money on health care. If we learned to consult the doctor within us, we could prevent much of our own disease. We would then live happier, more fulfilling lives and save money. Sickness of course causes many lost hours of work, so both national and global economies suffer. The body will often cure itself if we give it rest and proper nutrition. However, a meat-based diet inhibits the body's efforts to cure itself.

There is also a more critical connection between diet and economics. There is still, in the early 21$^{st}$ century, a lot of malnutrition and starvation in the world. The cost of one kilogram of meat protein is about twenty times higher than the cost of the same amount and quality of plant protein.

This difference concerns the use of land. If we give a steer one acre to graze on, the land will produce less than 1/2 kilogram of edible protein from the steer. If we planted soybeans in the same area, we can produce about 8 kilograms of edible protein.

Scientists calculate that raising animals for food uses eight times as much water as growing vegetables and grains for human consumption.

Jean Mayer, a nutritionist at Harvard University, estimates that reducing meat production by just 10% would release enough grain to feed 60 million people.

If you are new to vegetarianism, you may not know how to prepare a nutritious, tasty, vegetarian diet. Many books are available to help you and as you meet more vegetarian friends, you will pick up more and more ideas.

## Fasting

I've found it's very rewarding to know what to eat. It's also rewarding to know what not to eat. And when not to eat. Fasting (to abstain from food) is an important part of our lifestyle and has been throughout human history, even though it may not be practiced by so many people today. When we abstain from food we are holding to our will to not eat or drink for a long time. The time period, of course, is variable. Some people fast for one day. Others may fast for weeks. You may fast with no food or drink, or you may take some drink (and perhaps some food) but in very moderate, limited measure.

Since we eat every day, our digestive organs do not get a chance to rest and renew themselves. During our sleeping hours most of our body rests. Our eyes are closed, our lungs breathe more slowly, our legs and arms are at ease and our voice and ears are inactive. However, our intestines are still digesting the last meal. They rest only when they can stay without food for a long time.

For a person in normal health a fast can be most beneficial. It can increase not only your health, but also your longevity and mental strength.

Some of my students have suggested that the time between regular meals is a resting time for the digestive organs. During this period we may not feel the intestines working. However, they are then in full swing digesting the food from the previous meal and getting into gear, so to speak, to ingest and digest the next meal. A fast needs to be longer than the normal gap between meals.

I perform regular fasts for 24 to 36 hours. No food, no liquid. I rarely if ever over-eat the rest of the month. Thus, I eat a good deal less than a non-faster of similar habits. Yet I'm not at all underweight, nutritionally deficient or lacking in energy. I recommend everyone to fast twice a month. Try it for a few months and see what it does to improve your health. The best days to fast, according to the yogic system, relate to the cycle of the moon (as explained below). The dates for the current year are available from Ananda Marga yoga teachers or on an Ananda Marga website.

A small note: while regular fasting is beneficial to your health, a regular diet is also very beneficial. Fasting provides regular rest for your stomach. The stomach, though, will work best if it also has a regular rhythm of eating. Too much snacking during the day, combined with several meals, reduces the efficiency of the stomach in digesting food.

Fasting has a long history. People fast for mystical, ascetic, religious or ethical reasons, as well as for health. Members of certain Native American tribes fast as part of their preparation for a vision quest. People of the Jain religion fast to help them reach subtle levels of consciousness. Judaism has several fasting days in its annual calendar. Islam singles out the month of Ramadan for a daily fast from dawn to dusk.

Some people are well-known for their fasting. Buddha, in his intense search for enlightenment went on a long fast, before realizing it was too severe for his needs. Mila Repa, the most renowned Tibetan saint and poet, fasted for long periods, just drinking herbal concoctions.

You can gain more from fasting if you know how to conduct

the fast. While fasting itself is important, it is also very important to begin and end the fast properly. Some people think we should start a fast by eating a large meal. After all, we are not going to eat again for a long time. This not only can make the fast more difficult, but it can negate the effect of the fasting. When I first started to fast, I sometimes overate so much that I had no desire to eat for the next day or so. However, I don't call this a fast, because my intestines were working very hard the whole time processing what I dumped into them. They got no rest and sometimes tried to make sure I in turn got no rest, by inflicting a stomach ache on me.

It is better to start a fast by eating a light meal, or at most, a normal meal. Overeating before fasting can make you more thirsty than normal. If you are doing a dry fast, this thirst can be more disturbing than the lack of food. I also feel more hunger on a fasting day when I've overeaten the night before. In the yogic system, a fast goes from sunrise to sunrise.

The way you break the fast is just as important as the way you start it. Don't just grab a cup of coffee, some scrambled eggs and rush off to work or school. It's important to break a fast with plenty of liquid, especially if you have been doing a dry fast. A good way to break this type of fast is with a glass or two of lemon or lime water, with salt. You may also add some honey, for energy. This drink will neutralize the acidity of the stomach and flush out the intestines. I like to have a warm drink as I find it cleans out my intestines more thoroughly.

If you are new to fasting, you may be eager to break the fast, after taking sufficient liquid, with a large meal. This is no more beneficial than starting the fast after a large meal. Pouring a heavy meal into an empty stomach, which may have shrunk a bit from fasting, is a strain. It may cause a feeling of excessive heaviness for many hours, or a feeling of torpor, or, again, a stomach ache.

Better, after drinking lemon juice, wait a while, drink more liquid if you want, then have a light, digestible meal. Many people like to start their first meal by eating a ripe banana or two. It absorbs toxins and acids and helps bowel movements. Chew the banana very well. Enjoy it. Perhaps then you'll want to eat some more fruit, some yogurt. And, well... enjoy it, but stop eating sooner, rather than later.

Those who like to either start or end their fast with a big meal seem motivated more by desire than need. They are, perhaps, more hungry in the mind – or the tongue – than in the stomach. If we can control this desire, we will gain more mental strength and will power.

Your fasting can also be more beneficial if you fast on certain days. Yogic tradition recommends fasting on the eleventh day after the new and full moon. On these days the moon is at its closest point to the earth. The closer the moon is to the earth, the more gravitational pull it exerts on our planet. Humans have long observed that around the time of the full moon there is an increase in mental disturbance. Ask at a police station, as often at the time of the full moon more accidents and other problems are reported. It seems there is more lunacy when our lunar sphere is closer to the earth; ancient peoples were perhaps more aware than we are that the moon affects our behavior.

The moons' gravitation also affects the tides of the sea, creating stronger surges when the moon passes closer to the earth. Most of the human body is also liquid. On the days of heaviest lunar gravity the moon pulls the liquids of the body upward. Eating or drinking a lot on these days can cause a clogged feeling. Thus these days are most beneficial to fast.

You may think that fasting will cause you to waste your day, as you will not have so much energy. I find that if I pace myself I can get plenty of work done on a fasting day; sometimes more work than on other days. I first started fasting in my mid-20s. On those days, I could work a regular shift and often play basketball or volleyball afterwards. I had more time to enjoy meditation or to reflect on life because I wasn't busy preparing, eating and digesting three meals.

Hakeem Olajuwon was one of the best professional basketball players of the 1990s. As a Muslim, he fasts every day from sunrise to sunset during the month of Ramadan, which often falls during the basketball season. He also fasts on the other holy days of Islam. He recommends it to his professional colleagues. It does not hurt his game at all, he says. His fasting is not a 24 to 36-hour dry fast. Still, it is a long time to go without food or drink in such an intense occupation.

However, you may find you do feel hungry or tired. As I said, much of this is mental. The mind, as well as the body, has to adjust to the absence of the regular stimulation of eating. You may need to adjust your schedule, perhaps slow down a bit, or take a rest sometime during the day. The little bit of working time you may lose, however, is balanced by your overall increase in health.

Fasting may be undertaken for more than just physical health. Some use fasting to make a point. In modern times, for example, we often hear of fasting as a form of protest. Mahatma Gandhi often fasted to protest against the policies of the British, when they still controlled India. Dick Gregory, an American entertainer, often fasted, starting in the 1960s, to protest against social problems. He discovered that many health benefits resulted from fasting, along with the public attention he received for his causes. He wrote some widely respected books on the benefits of fasting and vegetarianism as a result of these experiences. We sometimes hear of prisoners fasting to protest against their conditions, or the very fact of their imprisonment.

Protest fasting serves to make people aware of the plight of the individual or of a group of people. It also has the effect of imparting more mental strength and will power to the person fasting. Increased mental strength also comes to people who fast for religious, ascetic or health purposes.

Voluntary fasting has other benefits too. It helps us to identify with the profound suffering of the hungry and starving people of the world. We should also try to help them. Ultimately this calls for us to change the global social and economic structure to enable all to enjoy the fruits of this bounteous planet.

Global changes such as these take a long time. However, there is at least something we can do now, while we work to ensure a decent living standard for all. Ananda Marga recommends that everyone who fasts should use the food money they save to feed the hungry.

Fasting has spiritual, as well as physical and mental, benefits. On fasting days, we have more time to think about our spiritual goal, as well as extending our consciousness toward the welfare of all beings, everywhere. So, though our stomachs may be empty on fasting days, our hearts and souls can fill up a little more.

## Sexuality and Spirituality

"Sex is at the root of life, and we can never know how to reverence life until we know how to understand sex."
— Havelock Ellis

"Love is that which helps us to understand the truth about ourselves and our possibilities."
— Jacob Needleman

The human quest for peace or happiness is often symbolized as a sense of union, between the seeker and the goal, between human and God, or between two lovers. They unite to become whole. Spiritually, one lover plus one lover do not become two lovers, but one complete lover or personality.

Humans often express this desire for union through sexuality. A loving sexual relationship can bring peace and happiness to oneself. Since sex also brings children, it is a creative act as well as an act of love.

Sexuality is part of our nature. So we need to have a natural, healthy, acceptable way to express it.

Too little, so to speak, is not healthy, but neither is too much. Too much sex can leave us worn out, in both body and mind. It can leave us feeling distant from our partner, and even feeling disconsolate. It can become more difficult to do meditation and practice other types of concentration.

Dr. Robert Assagioli notes that modern sexual liberation has eliminated some of the drawbacks of earlier, rigid attitudes about sexual expression. It has, however, produced other complications and conflicts. Excessive sexual activity, for example, often gives way to exhaustion. The sexual urge may also clash with our sense of self-preservation, since disease may often be the outcome of over-indulgence in sex.

Thus, both repression and uncontrolled gratification can bestow psychological or physical problems.

To solve the psychological problems, Gavin Harrison, a Buddhist monk and teacher, says, "Meditation practice enables us to be more aware of the intentions behind our sexual conduct." He suggests, "a period of restraint or celibacy may serve a deeper understanding of how sexual energy works in our life." Restraint, he notes, is different than repression, since restraint is a conscious choice.

Sexuality is not 'bad' or 'good.' It all depends on a person's motivation. A balanced approach would not support either repression or uncontrolled expression.

Assagioli suggests a multi-step process of transmutation and sublimation as a way to balance our sexual expression (though not to eliminate it). One type of transmutation is to direct our sexual desires inward toward a spiritual goal.

In a second type of transmutation we may substitute other pleasures for sexual pleasure. This may be food, enjoyment of nature, or other aesthetic pleasures.

At another stage, a person expands their feeling of love for the sexual partner so it includes more and more people. Eventually this love can include all people and all living creatures.

A third transmutation is creative or intellectual. The philosopher Arthur Schopenhauer notes that our higher creative energy is often aroused at the same time as our sexual drive. If we transmute the sexual energy into creative and spiritual energy, we can occupy ourselves with "the highest activities of the mind."

Assagioli suggests some psychological ways to transmute sexual energy to higher forms of expression. A conscious control of sexual drives, without condemnation or fear, is beneficial. It can be through physical means, including brisk muscular activity, rhythmic breathing, diet, etc. It can also be through accepting every human as our brother and sister, and not as an object of our gratification.

This sort of acceptance will increase gradually and can lead to an expression of love, not only toward our animate family, but also toward God.

We can also visualize or express (in art or writing for example) uplifting symbols. This may be in the form of ideal figures. A man may use the symbol of a hero or a human-divine being. He may also use the image of an ideal woman. A woman may visualize her highest ideal of womanhood, or the image of her ideal man.

Also helpful is communion with 'human catalysts,' that is, people with similar values or goals.

"The... drives which produce so much individual suffering and social disturbance can become, if rightly controlled and channeled, the springs of activities having great human and spiritual value."

What is a balance of sexual expression? There is no absolute answer to this. I believe present day popular psychology offers little clear guidance. Dr. Jacob Needleman notes: "...whatever service modern psychology has done by liberating us from the tyranny of sexual guilt is surely counterbalanced by its having led us more and more to define ourselves... in terms of sexual pleasure."

Try having sex four times a month, or less if you prefer. Many people will think this is just too little sex. Examine your sexual relationships. How much of your sexual expression is because of the need for sex and how much is just for ego satisfaction?

Sex education is important so we can grow up with a healthy view of what role sex can play in our lives.

Certain yogic asanas, and other practices, can help us to control our sexuality if we feel it is out of control.

For various reasons some people choose a celibate lifestyle. This is not a practical permanent solution to sexual confusion though. Even monks or nuns should not, I think, take up celibacy just because they are unsure of their sexuality. Short-term celibacy can be useful if you want to reflect on the role sex plays in your life. It can serve a bit like a fast, giving us time to stand back and see where our sexual life is going. Whether celibacy is temporary or permanent one has to find some way to balance the physical and psychic energy we associate with sexuality. If you repress these feelings they will find some way to express themselves. As a prisoner may try to sneak out of the window at night, so repressed feelings may sneak out of your mind without your control.

The physical disciplines of yoga are essential to help create harmony and self-control in each of us.

Chapter 4

# THE SPIRITUAL HIGHWAY:
# THE NATURE OF THE MIND

We are shaped by our thoughts; we become what we think.
When the mind is pure, joy follows like a shadow that
never leaves.
— Buddha

None but ourselves can free our minds.
— Bob Marley

Our mind is capable of passing beyond the dividing line we
have drawn for it. Beyond the pairs of opposites of which the
world consists, other, new insights begin.
— Hermann Hesse_

An emperor was coming out of his palace for his morning walk
when he met a beggar. He asked the beggar, "What do you
want?"

The beggar laughed and said, "You are asking me as though
you can fulfill my desire!"

The king was offended. He said, "Of course I can fulfill your
desire. What is it? Just tell me."

And the beggar said, "Think twice before you promise
anything."

The beggar was no ordinary beggar. He was the emperors past
life spiritual teacher. He had promised in that life, "I will come
and try to wake you in your next life. This life you have missed
but I will come again." But the king had forgotten completely;
who remembers past lives? So he insisted, "I will fulfill anything

88

you ask. I am a very powerful emperor. What can you possibly desire that I can not give to you?"

The beggar said, "It is a very simple desire. You see this begging bowl? Can you fill it with something?"

The emperor said, "Of course!" He called one of his ministers and told him, "Fill this man's begging bowl with money." The minister went and got some coins and poured it into the bowl, and it disappeared. And he poured more and more, and the moment he would pour it into the bowl, it would disappear. And the begging bowl remained always empty.

The whole palace gathered. People throughout the capital heard and a huge crowd gathered. The prestige of the emperor was at stake. He said to his ministers, "If the whole kingdom is lost, I am ready to lose it, but I cannot be defeated by this beggar."

Diamonds and pearls and emeralds were poured in; his treasury was becoming empty. The begging bowl seemed to be bottomless. Everything that was put into it immediately disappeared. As evening came the people stood there in utter silence. The king dropped at the feet of the beggar and admitted defeat. He said, "You are victorious, but before you leave, just tell me one thing: what is the begging bowl made of?"

The beggar laughed and said, "It is made up of the human mind. There is no secret. It is simply made of human desire."

While many human desires are for things of the world – money, food, fine clothing, and so much more – the desires themselves are expressing something of the mind. Naturally we do need comfort and security and much of this comfort is for the needs of the body. But beyond our normal needs, we often are hankering for things that we may want, but don't really need.

The nature of the mind is to want more. As Anandamurti says, "No one wants the want (the lack) of anything." But when we guide this insatiable desire – the begging bowl we just read about – towards finite goals, only toward things of the world, then the mind cannot be satisfied for long.

Of course we should not forget about the world, we should not repress or ignore our desires, for then they may find a way to bounce back to the forefront of our minds and disturb us more than the original desire.

Thus if one decides to live a life of solitary meditation or prayer, having little to do with the world, I daresay that this lifestyle will not last long if the person is simply trying to run away from desires. For while you may run away from your family, or job or home, away from people you don't like, or people you do like, you cannot run away from your mind, or what the mind desires.

Rather, let's find a way to direct the mind towards true fulfillment.

If the mind has decided to do something; the decision of the mind will usually override any rational thought we have on the subject.

I've gone through many years where I've had a lot of difficulty in controlling my mind and my emotions. I went through long periods where I would tell myself: 'be more in control' or 'don't let your mind wander.' These thoughts reflected what I needed in those days, to keep balance in my life. I just didn't have the mental strength or determination to follow this truth. As well, in those days I had no 'tools' to help me keep my mind together.

However, I eventually found that yogic guidelines helped me take the steps I needed, so I could gain this inner strength and find the balance I needed in my life.

I've often shied away from 'guidelines', thinking them to be too restrictive. However, yogic guidelines tend to be constructive. They add a structure to our lives that helps us to get along in life. They are not rules or dogmas that intend to restrict what we do or say or think.

There are at least three types of rules, guidelines, or laws that we follow in our life. There are natural laws. For example, if you put your hand into a fire, it will burn you. Another natural law is that if I eat proper food it will help me to be strong, healthy, and thus more effective in my life. The 'nature' or natural rule of a hurricane is that it can knock down virtually anything in its path when it's at full strength.

*Natural laws* can't be argued with. We must adjust our personal desires or attitudes to nature. It is natural to try to stay alive, and to try to stay healthy. Attitudes such as these seem to be programmed into living beings.

Natural laws are, of course, indiscriminate. A sage or a thief will both get burned by fire; both will starve if they don't eat.

As well, natural laws are not like a flea market, where you can pick and choose which ones you want in your life. What would happen to our world if, for example, glass windows sometimes let in light and other times didn't let in light? I wonder how our economy would function if we sometimes ate three times a day, and other times only once a week.

It's true that natural laws may not take into account our individual preferences. However, with a little effort and thought, we can live in harmony with natural laws and use them to our advantage.

There are also *social laws*. Cross the street with the green light. Pay your taxes. Go to school until a certain age. Don't steal. Don't murder.

Social laws, unlike natural laws, may be up for discussion. They do change from place to place and time to time. Humans are social creatures. We are also creatures of some free will. We each have our own mind on certain matters. So, we need to strike a balance between what we want and what the society wants, and we may have to limit or modify our behavior if it interferes with the rights of others.

Social laws have many purposes and one purpose is to govern or guide our interactions. Their role in our lives may not be as obvious as natural laws. They are more fluid, and some of these laws are open to the whim of the moment. And while social laws set norms on personal behavior, they are not as rigid or unchangeable as natural laws. Some social laws may seem to be more personal than social.

Traffic laws, for example, vary from place to place and may be enforced more or less strictly in different situations. Once, late at night in a state neighboring my home state, I was stopped for speeding. The policeman, in the course of checking out the car's registration and my identity got to know that I had lived and travelled in various countries on several continents. He then told me that he'd drop any charges if I would send him police badges from various places I travelled to. (Ultimately after checking out their records, all was fine and there were no charges to make against me, but his lenient attitude reflected how social laws are quite variable.)

So, though social laws regulate human behavior, they are not unchangeable. They also are not designed to help us understand how to interact with others, or how to find inner harmony.

There is a third level of law that is natural, but also conscious. It is social, but also psychological and universal. It is purposeful rather than imposing. It is constructive and dynamic. And it is timeless. In Sanskrit, this type of law is called *Niiti*. English words close to niiti would be morality or ethics.

According to Anandamurti, "Niiti (is) that which carries one towards a particular direction for one's good."

I tend to think of these guidelines as having been discovered, rather than invented or legislated, which is the case with social laws. The people who have found these guidelines seem to have explored deep levels of human consciousness. Part of the reason for Niiti is because human nature is so unpredictable. The things of this world may be used for good or bad, so we need some ideas on what is proper use of anything. Someone may use fire to cook their dinner, or, alternatively, to burn down someone's house. Steel can be used to make a building or a bullet.

The various guidelines of Niiti may be called *spiritual laws*. They are designed to help us channel our behavior toward constructive ends, both for our individual and social happiness.

The essence of Niiti is in two sets of complementary guidelines called *Yama* and *Niyama*. Yama means 'controlled contact with others' and Niyama means 'self-regulation.' They developed over many generations in ancient India. Much later, around 2,000 years ago, the sage, Patanjali, used these guidelines as the foundation for his system of *Astaunga Yoga*. This system is still followed to some degree by many yoga schools, including Ananda Marga.

Social laws, in theory at least, tell us what is best to do or not do for society. Those who developed Yama and Niyama studied what a society needs from its members and what the members need from society and from themselves. Yama and Niyama are guidelines for both individual and social human conduct

Social laws may help prevent bad or anti-social behavior, at least to some extent. Niiti is not only to stop bad behavior, but to help guide our actions and attitudes in a positive, benevolent way. For example, a social law or custom may discourage me from stealing, through fear of punishment. And while this fear may discourage me from stealing, it may not stop the desire to steal. If I want to stop both the habit and the mindset of stealing, I need to find a productive activity to replace this habit in my mind.

A story is told about a sage in ancient India named Kabir who was the minister of a great king. One day Kabir arrived at court and saw that one official had been found guilty of taking bribes. The king asked his ministers what to do with this man. Some insisted that if he were just given a job away from economic temptations he would be honest. Kabir doubted that this would work.

The king listened to his other ministers and decided to give the official a petty job away from money. So he was given the duty of sitting on the bank of a certain river, counting the waves, hour-by-hour, day-by-day.

For some days the king heard no complaint against the minister. Then Kabir suggested that he, the king and some others should visit the man. However, they should go disguised as common people, so they could better judge the man's true behavior.

They changed their dress, got in a boat and sailed down the river. After a while, they saw the official sitting in his assigned place. He was holding a notebook, putting marks in columns for low waves and high waves. "See," said one minister, "he's just doing his job." Kabir was silent.

As their boat came close to the official, he shouted: "Stop! Come here." So they pulled their boat over to the shore. "I am on an assignment from the king," he said, "to count the waves for an important inquiry. Anyone disturbing the flow of the waves will therefore have to pay a fine, which you must pay now. This is an order from the king."

This is an example of a social law that doesn't cure the problem; it just buries it.

## Universal Guidelines

Morality is the base of social life. It is also an effort to lead a balanced life. If we want happiness and harmony in our individual and social life, we must have mental balance. Morality is the effort to control the mind by controlling how we express ourselves.

I once read a story of an old Cherokee, describing to his grandson an experience going on inside himself.

"It is a terrible fight and it is between two wolves. One is evil: he is anger, envy, sorrow, regret, greed, arrogance, self-pity, guilt, resentment, inferiority, lies, false pride, superiority, and ego.

The other is good: he is joy, peace, love, hope, serenity, humility, kindness, benevolence, empathy, generosity, truth, compassion, and faith. This same fight is going on inside you, and inside every other person, too."

The grandson thought about it for a minute and then asked his grandfather: "Which wolf will win?"

The old Cherokee simply replied, "The one you feed."

Yama and Niyama are guidelines that were developed to suit human psychology and human nature. Yogis who developed these guidelines understood that the essence of human nature, of human motivation, doesn't change much from time to time or place to place. They looked deeply at themselves and at the societies of their times. They understood that there are laws that are above both nature and society.

So, some of the criteria for the guidelines of Yama and Niyama are that they are timeless, universal, constructive, positive, and balanced.

If the laws of society were based on Yama and Niyama, they would likely be less restrictive and more constructive. They would then help guide us to internal and social harmony.

As we explore the 10 steps of Niiti, I think we'll see that they fill in the gaps left by most present day social codes.

The English word, morality may make people feel a bit skittish or leery. It has a connotation of someone trying to impose their ideas on others. It seems to have a tinge of irrationality as well as imposition. "Thou shalt do what I tell you to do."

Indeed, moral rules based on coercion are dogmatic, because they limit our choices of rational behavior. From yogic viewpoints, they have nothing to do with morality.

Anandamurti says: "When... morality, on which the very existence of humanity is based, leads human beings to the fullest expression of their finer human qualities, then alone is its practical value fully realized."

The following sections deal with each of the ten points of Yama and Niyama. They are, though, not distinct entities. They all tie together. The ensuing discussion won't be exhaustive, nor,

I hope, exhausting. You may have a lot of questions, comments and stories to share on any of these points.

## Yama

1) *Ahimsa*: Ahimsa means *non-injury*. It is important to remember that your motivation for doing something is often as important as what you do. And though your actions, thoughts or words may not be intentionally harmful, if done without forethought, they may cause harm.

The Buddha says:

"All beings tremble before violence.
All fear death.
All love life.
See yourself in others.
Then whom can you hurt?
What harm can you do?
He who seeks happiness
By hurting those who seek happiness
Will never find happiness."

If we want to eliminate this attitude of harming others, then it's best to start before the idea, or attitude, of harmfulness has taken root in the mind. Nip it in the bud, as they say. It may be hard, though, to see these negative ideas growing in the mind. You can observe yourself in various ways to see if harmfulness is growing in yourself. Try to tune into your thoughts. Notice what you talk about. Do you express a lot of anger or vengefulness in your conversations? These can be signs of some imbalance you need to tend to.

If I do catch such thoughts or actions in myself, what can I do to resolve them? I can best make a negative mindset disappear by diverting it to a useful, or neutral, channel.

Physicists say that opposites attract. Can this work in

psychology? Buddha says: "Overcome anger by patience, overcome dishonesty by honesty, overcome greed by generosity, overcome falsehood by truth."

This means to put the opposite thought into a person's mind, when they are dominated by some negative idea. Of course, it may not be so easy. We may have to help the person to work through a lot of psychic traumas. They may not be willing to change, or even to accept that there is a problem. So we may, if we still care to help the person, need to be the active partner in this healing process.

Buddha's statement encapsulates a basic strategy. If you meet a miser, you cannot force him to be charitable. Rather, Buddha suggests that YOU can be charitable. Your example may influence the miser, gradually. If he does change, it may, at least at the beginning, be out of desire, not service. He may see that people are praising you, smiling at you and in turn helping you. He may want the same. Even if this is a selfish reason to start charity, still it's better than miserliness. We can hope that charity will become a habit in him and the inner greed will fall away. After some time, when the habit of charity gets established, he may truly take on the identity of being charitable.

A Zen story illustrates the point of counteracting negative behavior, rather than reacting to it:

There once lived a great warrior. Though quite old, he still was able to defeat any challenger. His reputation extended far and wide throughout the land and many students gathered to study under him.

One day an infamous young warrior arrived at the village. He was determined to be the first man to defeat the great master. Along with his strength, he had an uncanny ability to spot and exploit any weakness in an opponent. He would wait for his opponent to make the first move, thus revealing a weakness, and then would strike with merciless force and lightning speed. No one had ever lasted in a match with him for long.

Much against the advice of his concerned students, the old master gladly accepted the young warrior's challenge. As the two squared off for battle, the young warrior began to hurl insults at the old master. He threw dirt and spit in his face. For hours he verbally assaulted him with every curse and insult he knew. But the old warrior merely stood there motionless and calm. Finally, the young warrior exhausted himself. Knowing he was defeated, he left feeling shamed.

Somewhat disappointed that he did not fight the insolent youth, the students gathered around the old master and questioned him. "How could you endure such indignity? How did you drive him away?"

"If someone comes to give you a gift and you do not receive it," the master replied, "to whom does the gift belong?"

Some people ask me if non-injury means we should turn the other cheek, if someone hits us, so they can then slap us on that cheek too. When we allow someone to continue with anti-social behavior we are encouraging it. If you let someone slap you, just to avoid a bigger fight, then your actions tell him that he can continue to hurt whoever he wants. By avoiding some fighting, it may cause more harm to more people in the long run. So we may need to use force to stop actions that would otherwise lead to more damage.

Yoga psychology sees a big difference between force and harm, or injury. We use force every time we take a step. We may be killing many insects when we walk. We don't have much choice though.

Even when we do have a choice we need to look at the overall effect. For example, you may need to force a child to stop running across the street, because he doesn't look out for cars. A waiter or bartender may need to force a customer to stop drinking when the customer loses his self-control. It may be proper to use force to stop a government from detonating nuclear bombs, or from planting land mines. In cases of impending danger, there may not be time to talk quietly and rationally to someone who may be unable to see any danger. The force used in any of these circum- stances may be verbal or physical and may even hurt the person. It is acceptable force if it prevents a greater injury.

However, what if your effort to do good is motivated by anger or hatred? As we know, what we do is controlled by the mind, by our motivation. So if you stop your daughter from running across the street, by angrily yelling at her and beating her, she may well get a different message than your words convey. She may conclude that it's best not to tell Mom or Dad what she's going to do.

In sum, then, forceful action can be taken to correct a person. However, it should only be taken with the spirit and attitude of helping that person. Anandamurti says we have no right to punish someone we don't love.

Most of these examples deal with individuals. In a broader social context there are certain 'human enemies'. These people must be stopped at all costs. These 'human enemies', according to yogic principles, are those who take another's property, abduct or kidnap others, threaten murder with a weapon, burn another's house or property or attempt to poison another. These enemies can be individuals or groups.

Maybe the general or politician who threatens to invade your country started out by threatening his schoolmates. He should have been stopped and properly guided as a youth.

So, it is not against ahimsa to use force, to achieve a peaceful end.

So far we've talked about stopping bad actions. Beyond stopping it, we want to transmute it into good actions. This can be done. It depends on our goal in any situation.

Stephen Covey talks about the "Six paradigms of human inter-action." These paradigms or models are: win/win, win/lose, lose/win, lose/lose, win and win/win or No Deal.

Win/win of course means that both sides in any interaction get what they want, or need. As Covey says, this means we are not looking just to win for ourselves: "It's not your way or my way; it's a better way, a higher way."

Win/lose obviously means that I get what I want, and you don't get what you want; in most situations, this model would seem to be undesirable.

Can win/win be used to, say, stop a burglar? If I stop him then society has won, though he's lost. However, in the spirit of non-injury I would try to help the burglar take up an honest, productive profession. In this example, the attitude of the society is important. If our jails only punish criminals, but offer them no education and no methods by which they can understand the negative effects of their behavior, then criminality won't decrease. An important part of ahimsa is to change the negative motivation of a person.

This positive view of ahimsa leads us to the second point of Yama.

2) *Satya*: Satya is the action of mind and the right use of words with *the spirit of welfare*. I see it as a step beyond ahimsa – non-injury. Ahimsa is a good starting point in our relations with others. However, we also need to have a positive motivation in our lives. Yoga psychology sees that this motivation needs to be something more than what I want out of life, for myself.

When one thinks only of their own welfare, the results may be unexpected, at the least, or even disastrous.

An example is a short story I once read, about a man of 48 years, who had met a sort of sorcerer who gave him a boon. The sorcerer blessed the man by saying that as long as he was alive the man would stay as young and healthy as if he were 48 years old. This was satisfying to the man, who envisioned himself staying at a healthy middle-age, even while all his friends and relatives grew old. He told his wife that night about the blessing he'd received and she urged him not to forget her when he saw this sorcerer again. She didn't want to grow old while her husband stayed the same age, year after year. The husband assured her in a self-satisfied way that he would do that, when he next saw the sorcerer.

And in the morning, the husband was dead; the blessing of the sorcerer was fulfilled, as he had kept the health and appearance of a 48 year old as long as he was alive.

The writer of the story depicted a husband who meant no harm, but whose attitude was selfish and went against nature; in this way he was ultimately self-destructive.

Satya is an active principle that gives us a general sense of something positive to do in any situation.

Ever wonder why so many criminals go back to jail after they've served their first sentence? Is it just because they're no good? Perhaps society protected itself in the short term by putting some thief or murderer in jail. Did this stop the problem though?

If we prevent crime, this may be the spirit of non-injury, as it will protect others from that person, while they are in jail. However, if we don't adopt the spirit of satya in dealing with prisoners, we'll always be stopping the same people from committing more crimes.

An example of how to use Satya for a criminal would be to help him learn something constructive and humane. While society demands punishment for a crime, we also need to ask: what is the best thing that society can do for those in prison? Logically, their basic needs are the same as everyone else and education or job training can help to minimize future crime.

Satya can also mean relative truth. Sometimes literal truth hurts more than it helps. What if a neighbor of yours comes to hide in your house, to avoid someone who she claims is an abusive partner? If that man then comes to your place, looking for the partner, would you follow absolute truth (which might also be called 'simple morality') and tell him that the woman is in your house? Though you may not really know if the person is abusive, it would be safer, in the short run, to simply say that you don't know where she is.

This idea of relative truth is not recommended simply for one's own convenience. I once read about two secondary school students who always drove to school together, in one of the students' car. They had an exam one day that neither of them felt ready for. So they delayed their trip, arriving after the exam was well under way. They told the teacher that they had had a flat tire and that's why they were late.

The teacher looked at them, nodded and arranged for them to come in at another time to take the exam. They were put in separate rooms and each of them had a paper with one simple question on it: "Which tire was flat?"

Satya also has a philosophical meaning. It refers to both relative and absolute truth. This idea is that the relative world, the universe we live in, is a microcosm or representation of absolute truth. In this sense, we follow satya when we try to harmonize our thoughts and actions with universal truth.

3) *Asteya*: If we develop the attitude of Satya, it helps us to establish Asteya in our heart and mind. Asteya means *non-stealing*, or not to take possession of what belongs to others. However the essence of asteya is not just to refrain from stealing, but to have your mind and heart free from any concept of, or desire for, theft.

Anandamurti lists four types of stealing. These include:

- *Physical theft*. Whether by stealth, violence or deceit, it is still theft.

- *Mental desire to steal.* You may not steal just because you are afraid to get caught. However, if the idea is still in your mind then this wave keeps churning, keeps unbalancing the mind. Eventually the wave will have to either calm down or get so big that it finally leads you to steal.

- *To deprive others of what is due them,* or to avoid paying what you owe. A scholar may publish a paper but 'forget' to give credit to his research assistants. Or your boss writes a letter of commendation, for work well done, to a fellow employee. He asks you to give it to her. You somehow just leave it in your desk, never giving it to her, perhaps because you are jealous of her receiving such a letter. Or you travel by public transport without buying a ticket. After all, you may think, what do they need my few coins for? I'm not really taking anything from them, just a bit of space.

The social harm of these actions may be insignificant. However, if it makes the 'steal' waves bigger in your mind, then it will also encourage fear to seep more into your mind. You know you've done something wrong, though no one else may know it. Indeed, it may be impossible ever to catch you. When you get off the train at your station, who can ever know you didn't buy a ticket? And perhaps the research assistant was paid for his work, and technically he can't complain that his name didn't appear in the book, even though he had done a lot of the work.

Still, your mind is affected. You know you could have done better than you did, could have been a bit more honest or generous.

- A fourth form of theft is *to mentally desire or plan to deprive others.* Again, no social harm is done here. But the more we think about it, the closer those waves keep splashing to the shore of action. In a subtle level, also, these desires affect the way we act with others. Our relationships and our self-image suffer.

Stealing, like injuring, originates in the mind. We can either nurture these seeds of theft or injury or we can throw them into a sort of psychic dustbin.

Although most of us do not steal, we may desire to have what belongs to someone else. Social controls train us not to act on these feelings. We may, though, have the attitude that the grass is always greener on the other side.

Thus, your mind may be bursting with emotions such as greed, anger, hate or jealousy. Most people don't know how to either express or eliminate such feelings. We may just think: "How do others control all these feelings?"

Somehow most of us keep our stronger, more violent emotions inside. We don't steal or injure others. At least in our actions and words we've adapted to the mores of the society.

It seems to me there are undercurrents in society where unresolved emotions do cause great problems. No, most of us are not stealing or killing. However, many adults are taking a lot of pills or smoking and drinking too much. We divorce and remarry, we may not feel that we have enough friends, or enough time to spend with the family, and, well, the list of our discontent goes on and on.

In many countries, this type of 'living' is accepted as the norm. As a teacher of meditation, though, I don't accept that this excessive nervousness, tension, frustration and physical illness should be the fate of humanity.

Our psychic problems represent distortions in the mind which sometimes seem to have a mental life of their own. For example: do you ever find yourself humming a song you don't like? I've had this happen many times, and if I want to get rid of that tune I can't just say, "Go away." So, whether my nemesis is bad music or hate, fear, envy, etc. it may not disappear just because I want it to. That is, I can't just repress the thoughts.

I can, however, channel my thoughts and actions to safe outlets, or try as Buddha suggested, replacing negative with positive thoughts. It's of course not always easy to know how to 'delete' all the negative stuff from our minds. Some of these emotions can be channeled positively by engaging in social service. Perhaps you've learned sign language so you can help deaf people in some way, or you know computer or wilderness skills, which you can teach to young people. In one way or another, you can replace your fear or greed with satisfaction that you helped someone. Someone benefited from your good actions.

As we engage in more and more constructive work, the satisfaction we feel from doing this good work will fill our minds, leaving little room up there for our negative or destructive emotions.

These are examples of creating a positive wave in the mind to balance out the negative wave. In these ways, some of our mental turbulence can be eased.

If you want to resolve problems of anger, greed, etc., then you may also need counseling, or at least someone you can talk openly to. Meditation can of course help. Regular meditation helps you dig deeper and deeper into your mind and heart. You may uncover uncomfortable feelings or fears that have been buried there for a long time; when you bring them to the light of day, to the top of your mind, you can do something about them.

To dissolve these distortions we must first recognize we have them. Meditation is one tool to help us dissolve them, or channel them into good work.

4) *Brahmacharya*: This means to remain attached to, or to identify ourselves with, Brahma, Supreme Consciousness. There are two practical ways that we do this. One way is, according to a yogic formula, to think of Brahma throughout the day.

The other method is to see all people and other objects as expressions of Brahma. For some of us this may seem ridiculous. After all, if I see everyone as Brahma, that is, as part of my family, does this mean I have to love terrorists, or the person who stole my car radio?

Well, yes. Love is the motivating force in the universe,

though, saying that, I can also say that love is not just to smile and say everything is beautiful. If there is conflict between people, yoga emphasizes the need for a permanent solution, such as Covey's 'win/win'. It may be easy for you to stew in anger and frustration. It may be much harder to sit down with your enemies and express real needs and hopes to each other. This is courageous. It is also an act of love. It means we care enough about the other person that we may be willing to give up something we want, to find a greater peace. It also means that we are willing to talk to the 'other', the perceived enemy or antagonist, and directly communicate our needs and feelings, and listen to their needs and feelings.

Peace, though, cannot be based on just giving the other guy what he wants, since if I am giving in to others all the time, this may just reflect my own mental weakness. Conversely, if I always get what I want I may become selfish and lazy. I may also lose my concern for the welfare of others. Thus I'll lose my sense of ahimsa, satya and asteya. On a global level, this attitude will probably dampen any interest I have in achieving real peace, since peace between individuals, or between nations, usually involves some compromise. Real peace means fairness and friendliness.

Brahmacharya, then, means we want to treat everyone as if they are part of our family. In a healthy family the brothers and sisters see each other as equally valuable, not as inferior or superior. Each contributes what they can to the family and naturally everyone helps each other. Family members may argue with each other, but at the end of the day they try to resolve their problems.

In the Ananda Marga meditation system, the first and second lessons are important tools to help us establish the feeling of Brahmacharya, of universal kinship.

5) *Aparigraha*: This is the effort to control one's tendency for

greed and attachment. It is both a social and an individual process. It relates closely to Brahmacharya and to Santosha, which we'll discuss later. It also relates closely to ecology. And to peace.

According to Anandamurti, what we really want in life is peace, or composure. We can't have this without proper health, which includes food, clothing, housing and other factors. However, if we are always looking for more and more, desiring one million pound sterling when £100,000 is quite enough, then we also lose our peace of mind.

James Allen says: "You will become as small as your controlling desire; as great as your dominant aspiration."

This describes how *'parigraha'*, that is, 'specific taking' or greed, affects us in our personal life. We lose our peace of mind either by taking too much or not having enough. The society can do something to stop individual greed. Certain standards of consumption can be set. There can be a limit on the number of cars or houses or land that a person or family can own (depending on the size of the family and other needs). A fair system of taxation can do something to prevent over-accumulation.

However, laws alone can't eliminate greed. If we punish people whom we define as greedy, we won't solve the problem. To help greedy people recover mental balance some form of psycho-therapy may be needed.

Ultimately, aparigraha depends on the individual. Social pressures, though, may be necessary to encourage unselfishness. However, besides 'pressure,' we can take positive steps by, for example, educating students to the benefits of simple living.

Meditation can of course help one to overcome greed. One aspect of meditation that helps us in this way is that we develop a sense of unselfishness. This happens at least partly because of a feeling of inner security and partly because of a feeling of being part of one universal family. Naturally, then, we wish to 'share and share alike.'

While the global ecological movement grasps some of the dangers of over-accumulation and waste, few ecologists or economists articulate a comprehensive approach to simple living. People accept and desire many unnecessary conveniences that lead directly and indirectly to air and water pollution, countless tons of unrecyclable waste and ozone holes.

If we think seriously about aparigraha, and its implications for our personal and world-wide well-being we can take active steps to save the earth. Such steps as recycling, using less water, electricity and fuel, and eating a vegetarian diet give us more than just material gains. According to Anandamurti, we gain some psychic ease by reducing "our own comfort out of sympathy for the common people."

The way we apply aparigraha will vary from place to place and time to time. For example, in a poor country, not every one can afford a car. In such cases, where there is a severe shortage, the more rare and special items should go to those who can utilize them best for the society. It's reasonable for a doctor to have a car in such a situation, so she can visit sick people and perform her duties better.

A brief review of the other principles of Yama shows that they all connect to aparigraha. Wastefulness or greed injures others. It goes against a sense of thinking and acting for others welfare. It is, in a sense, stealing comfort from others, both now and in the future (and from the whole physical world). If we truly see every being as part of our family, we naturally try to use all resources properly so others don't suffer from our greed.

All five principles of Yama are, in a sense, just different parts of one whole. While they deal with different aspects of human nature, they all have a similar goal: to help us move toward a peaceful, progressive society and a peaceful mind.

You can do several things to develop one or more of these points in yourself. Look at your life objectively. Study this chapter and other literature on Yama and Niyama. You may see a gap between your actions now and the ideal of how you want to live. If so, take steps, perhaps with the help of a friend or teacher, to improve your 'performance' in these points.

## Living Your Life

Late one night, in fact well after midnight one summer evening in 1983, I was driving with three friends. We'd left Kansas City that afternoon and were hoping to get to Indianapolis, a good half-day or more travel, by early morning. We would go to our friends' house there, then rest, bathe, do our morning meditation practice, have breakfast and be on our way so that we could – hopefully – reach our destination, Washington DC, by late evening.

Along the way, we had some car trouble on a rural road in southern Illinois. It was an area far off the beaten path of any yogis (as we would have described ourselves) that I'd ever known.

We stopped in a petrol station. Three of us started looking into the problems of the car, plus taking care of some other odds and ends that would make our travels more comfortable. We were eager to be on the road again, keeping in mind our proposed arrival time in Indianapolis (which was still several hours drive ahead of us). Meanwhile, our fourth companion, Michael, took it on himself to engage the station attendant – a small town fellow of perhaps 19 or 20 years old – in a long conversation about yoga, the meaning of life and related topics.

While three of us were in a hurry, we couldn't pull Michael away from his conversation with this young man from this backwater area of the Bible Belt.

I felt it would be impossible, or at least highly

improbable, for Michael to interest this fellow in yoga, mysticism or spiritual matters. But then, as I was passing by them, on my way toward checking the oil or water, or whatever I was doing, I heard the young man say something that has stuck with me ever since. In one sentence he seemed to sum up much of what 20<sup>th</sup> century philosophy, sociology and psychology had spent countless volumes writing about. He said to Michael: "Sure, I believe in God and all that, but you gotta live your life too."

I was too busy then with the engine (or was it the tires?) to dwell on his comment, or to join the conversation, but later I realized that this young man was simply describing the confusion that modern people feel as we try to find meaning in life, as we try to connect our fragmented selves with a yogic (in the sense of unified, or integrated) life that I believe we all wish to have.

Oh, we did make it to Indianapolis on schedule, had a refreshing few hours there and were each asleep in our own beds in Washington DC later that night.

## Niyama

The five items of Niyama concern self-regulation. If I want to be free in life, I must have inner strength and awareness. Strength comes from self-control. There are of course many other ways to find freedom, but inner strength is a fundamental step toward freedom. The five points of Niyama are guideposts to help us determine our inner strength and awareness.

1) *Shaocha*: This refers to physical cleanliness and mental purity. Both the body and mind need to be clean and pure. If I'm dirty, my physical health will suffer. Physical cleanliness refers not only to my body but also to my surroundings.

If my outer life is clean and in order, it's likely my inner life will be the same. The inner and outer seem often to reflect each other. Inner cleanliness is both physical and mental. A sick body doesn't usually 'just happen.' It's likely that something we've done, or failed to do, has contributed to our sickness.

Physical sickness often relates to mental imbalance. Poor eating habits can reflect a disregard of yourself. It can also reflect disregard of others. Meat-eating, for example, is generally not healthy for people, and as well, reflects a disregard for other living beings.

Purity or cleanliness of the mind is, like physical purity, both inner and outer. Outer mental purity may be hard to understand. It refers to external stimuli that affect our mind. A sculpture by Michelangelo may create subtle vibrations in our mind. These vibrations may make us yearn more to know the truth in life. This is an example of external mental purity.

Pornography is an example of external mental 'dirt'. It is something we see that creates negative images in our mind. If we are attracted to pornography our mind becomes more dirty or impure and this will affect our behavior.

Internal mental purity is affected, for better or worse, by our memories. Something you do today may trigger a memory from years ago. If that action triggers a memory of Michelangelo, fine. If it triggers a memory of pornography, your mind will move further away from acceptable behavior.

When we are affected by physical or mental dirt, we need to clean it. Force is required in both cases. If I want to clean my body, my clothes or my house I need to scrub with soap, water and a brush. It means, of course, that we need to come in contact with dirt. We may even need to seek dirt out to make our house or body cleaner. We must find it before we can dispose of it.

When we clean our mind we don't need to come in contact with dirt. We just need to replace it with purity. As a dirty mind is generally harder to clean than a dirty body, it's better if we can keep it 'dirt-free' from the start.

This is not always possible. If you grow up in a community where it's common for people to drink, fight or steal then you may develop the same habits. However, later in life you may meet people who inspire you to lead a more pure, honest life. Even if you are attracted to this new lifestyle you may still be affected by the memories and habits of your youth, which have created certain patterns in your mind, and this may make it hard for you to take up the new lifestyle.

You need to use mental force to clean out this dirt. Some application of Buddha's formula of opposites, noted above, can be very useful. It's not enough to say, "No, I don't want to continue with this behavior." This statement is a good start. However, after you determine that you don't want a certain habit, you need to replace it with something.

There are various ways to bring a good habit into the mental space of a bad habit. A smoker, for example, may study the bad effects of tobacco. It won't be long before he's seen enough pictures of cancer victims wasting away, losing vital organs while their skin and teeth turn some sickly shade of yellow or grey. This can provide a vivid picture to replace any mental vacuum that cigarettes had formerly filled.

He can also try to associate with non-smokers. This may involve starting some activity, such as sports or meditation, where the participants are not likely to be smokers.

Whatever 'bad' habits we are talking about, I think it's useful to try not to think about the habit very much. Of course, time and place may make a difference. A married couple I know became vegetarians but couldn't persuade their four and six year old sons to join them. So they took them on a tour of a slaughterhouse one afternoon. The boys, now adults, are still vegetarians.

The method may seem a bit too forceful. However, sometimes we must decide which type of suffering is greater. The parents I just mentioned took much time to try to fill the boys' minds with subtle, spiritual ideas. They must have felt that the health and welfare of their children was worth the possible traumas they might face from the memories of one afternoon of slaughter.

The mind controls behavior, and thus health. However, you can decide to emphasize either mental or physical cleanliness first. Somehow they reinforce each other.

2) *Santosha*:
"Once thrown off its balance, the heart is no longer its own master."
— St. Francois de Sales

Santosha means contentment, or a state of proper mental ease. This may not be as easy to define as, say, non-stealing, or non-injury.

It may help us to understand what contentment is if we look at its opposite. Discontentment, for example, may come from greed. In fact, one effective way to put contentment into your life is to practice aparigraha.

If you find that it's hard to hold onto mental calmness or contentment, then this contentment is probably not based on a deep inner sense of fulfillment.

Contentment or lack of contentment is not necessarily related to one's wealth. For example, ask a millionaire how she's doing. She may say: "Oh, just getting by, that's all." And the person may really feel that they are not doing so well economically. They aren't really in any economic danger, though. In this example I'd guess that the person's desire for wealth is driven by greed, not need. As this greed increases, both mental and physical health often deteriorate. High-tech doctors may patch up the physical problems for a while. The mental problems of greed, discontentment or loneliness are not so easy to repair.

What any person requires are the basic necessities of life. These include food, clothing, shelter, health and education. As well, each person needs santosha.

The human mind tends, in a way, to take the form of whatever occupies it. If you once encountered a fearsome dog, for example, that image may stay in your mind for a long time. Some people may develop a fixation on the image or memory of that fearsome dog and may find that they are afraid of dogs even years later.

While a greedy person may see everything in terms of its economic value they will probably find that accumulating wealth doesn't bring them happiness.

Material things are limited. They change form, they wear out, get torn or stale. They also lose their ability to attract us, to give us pleasure. I see that many people use money, a good meal or designer jeans just to run away from recurring boredom or loneliness. However, these pleasures always wear out or become less attractive to us. Then of course we just look for more of it, or something about the same but newer, different, perhaps more expensive. And the happiness is always just around the corner. It's never quite in your hand, nor in your heart.

Unlike money in the bank, it's hard to measure how much santosha we have. We can't stockpile or save it. But there may be ways to know if we do have true contentment. For example, are you unhappy when you see someone receive something, such as a birthday gift or a promotion at work? When you receive a gift do you wish you'd gotten more? If you do feel this way, then you need to develop more santosha.

There is a story about a couple with very little santosha, but a good deal of miserliness.

There was a tight-fisted man, named Soma, whose wife, Somii, was just as miserly. One day, when Soma returned home, his face was pallid and he was physically sick. Seeing his wretched condition, Somii asked:

'Soma, my darling, why is your face so pale? Why do you look so haggard? Have you lost some money? Did you happen to give a present to someone by mistake? Something like this must have happened, otherwise why would you look so pale?'

Soma replied: 'No, nothing like that. Neither have I lost any money, nor have I given a gift to anyone. I just happened to see someone giving a donation to another person and lost my usual composure.'

The practice of aparigraha, simple living, is a sort of gateway to santosha. If you are not satisfied, even though you have the material things you need, then perhaps you are not expressing some inner need of yours.

Passivity should not be confused with santosha. In fact, it is important that we fight to establish our legitimate rights, and those of others. If someone borrows £10 from you and you later realize they're not going to pay it back, should you just say, "Oh, why bother? Why get disturbed about it?" If this is your attitude, perhaps you are hiding some fear or cowardice. Of course this attitude also encourages the cheater to continue to cheat you and others.

On the material level, if you have a decent livelihood and still don't have a state of contentment, what can you do to get it? Learn to identify yourself with your true divine nature. Meditation of course helps with this.

There are some exercises you can also practice to help gain santosha. One type of exercise is auto-suggestion. Identify your negative or limiting tendencies. Then identify the opposite of these. Try to always think this opposite, more positive, thought.

If I find the problem is a personality defect then I can take the opposite viewpoint. Am I, for example, a selfish person, who repels people because I never give of myself in friendships? Then I can develop the idea in my mind that I like to give to others and that I always get what I need from others. I should fill my mind with this idea and act upon it so it does become part of my reality. Perhaps I can find a charity or service group through which I can help others. It's possible that I developed selfishness because I feared that others are taking from me, cheating me in some way. So if I regularly keep a self-image of being generous, I will gradually bring that attitude into my life.

3) *Tapah:*
   "Behold, I do not give lectures or a little charity.
   When I give, I give myself."
   — Walt Whitman

Tapah indicates service. However, in Tapah, there is a special tone to service. It means that we undergo, or are willing to undergo, sacrifice or hardship to help others.

Not all service qualifies as tapah. When a poor woman gives £10 to a charity, this may be tapah, because it is a lot of money for her. However, a rich person may have no trouble to give £1000. And while it is no doubt a useful service, little or no sense of difficulty or sacrifice may have been involved.

It is good to do service even if it's not tapah. There are many levels of service. I may sit for an hour to talk to a lonely man, helping to fill a bit of empty space for him. This is a relatively small service. However, if I go further in trying to help him, perhaps by encouraging him to resolve his inner problems, so he may overcome his loneliness, this is a greater service. It comes closer to tapah also, since I'm putting out considerably more effort to help him.

Tapah, though, is not just for the beneficiary. When I go to some trouble or sacrifice to help others, then I can identify with their problems. This brings me closer to the human heart. It helps me identify with the whole human race and may well increase my sense of compassion. It purifies my heart. "Self-sacrifice," said Ralph Waldo Emerson, "is the real miracle out of which all the reported miracles grow."

The essence of Tapah is, according to Anandamurti, "to shoulder sorrows and miseries of others to make them happy, to free them from grief and to give them comfort."

Henry Ward Beecher said: "In this world it is not what we take up, but what we give up, that makes us rich." So, in a sense I can derive personal benefit from tapah. However, if that is my motivation at the time of the service then I'm engaging in business, not service or tapah.

Anything I get that is worthwhile in this world requires some effort from me. It may only be the effort of opening my heart to others. Even this effort seems hard for many of us. Distrust, fear and ignorance often keep us apart from others in our human family. When I sacrifice something to really help someone, I'm also tearing down the artificial barriers between us.

In any service, our main responsibility is to those who are weaker or less fortunate than us. Everyone needs some sort of help. It may be economic, educational, psychological or something else. However, we have limited time in this life. So let's help those who have the most pressing problems and who are least able to pay for professional help.

4) *Svadhyaya*: This means to have a clear understanding of any spiritual subject.

This can take various forms. You may read a spiritual book and study the meaning of the writing; or you may listen to a respected commentator and try to understand what they say, and to understand if it is correct. If you really want to learn about spirituality, it's not enough to just read through a book and get a general idea of the author's narration. It's also not enough to have a great memory and be able to recite the text by rote. You need to understand the words, and try to apply them in your life.

Meditation helps us understand spiritual books. This is because in meditation we develop our intuition. This sixth sense is not just something that helps us know when the phone is going to ring, or when our close friend is going to have an accident. That is, intuition is not just the ability to foresee the future.

These last two examples suggest that intuition is a quick or immediate perception. However, it's also deep perception. In an earlier chapter I talked about symbols. Writers on spiritual or mystical subjects often use language and images with various levels of meaning. This symbolism was a sort of hide and seek exercise, wherein those with insight, or intuition could understand the subtle meaning. Profound writings can be read on various levels, each level of which is valid. The two most common levels are simply internal and external.

In the *Bhagavad Gita* Krishna tells Arjuna, a great warrior, that he must fight against his relatives and friends, no matter how repulsive such an idea would be to Arjuna. The outer meaning is that if someone wants to hurt you then you have the right, even the duty, to stop him or her, by any means necessary.

The inner meaning is that each of us is filled with both good and bad qualities. Don't let the bad qualities develop. Rather, "kill" them, replace them with good qualities. This we talked about earlier, when we discussed Shaocha and Santosha. As Arjuna was naturally unwilling to fight against his family and friends, in the same way we may be unable to see that certain parts of our personality are actually holding back our spiritual progress and our harmonious relations with others.

Spirituality is the endeavor to find ultimate truth. The physical sciences, arts, history, social sciences, grammar, etc., are relative truths. Certain recognized rules govern the use of these disciplines. However, they do change from time to time. History, for example, can be reinterpreted according to new evidence, or according to the viewpoint of each historian. Newton's analysis of universal physical laws was surpassed by Einstein, who had more information to work with, and Einstein's great discoveries are being supplanted by scientists with more information at their disposal.

Spirituality is not a physical phenomenon and is not a changeable phenomenon. (Granted, though, people express spiritual truths in different ways, according to the different times and places that they have lived.) It is also not measurable in the ways that we measure most things in the world. So to measure or find spirituality requires different instruments than those you would need to, say, design a new printing press, or a new telephone. To find spirituality we need the mind. However, since spirituality is not physical the mind has to use mental instruments to 'find' spirituality. One instrument is meditation. Another one is svadhyaya.

If, for example, I want to measure my spiritual progress, I can use my own perceptions and experience. Spiritual books also help me to measure my progress according to some acceptable norms.

I can, for example, compare my actions and thoughts to the ideals of Yama and Niyama. When we can establish ourselves in these universal ideals we can enter into deeper realms of spiritual awareness. Likewise, as we approach spiritual awareness each of us will find that we are following these principles more easily.

These measurements of spirituality are not concrete or measurable by normal standards. They depend both on how we live our life and on an inner feeling.

However, we should try to understand spiritual subjects before accepting them in our life.

One reason this is important is because there have been many misinterpretations of spirituality by so-called 'religious professionals.' This is a term that Anandamurti uses. These are people who have a stake in making us believe their interpretation of a spiritual teaching. They may discourage us from studying spiritual books in depth or from consulting teachings contrary to their own interpretation.

Many people in the world today are divided by religious doctrines and it seems that religious professionals encourage these artificial divisions. They have, for example, used their scriptures to condone death and torture of those outside their own fold.

Some young Muslim men have been persuaded that if they carry out suicide missions against their enemies, they will go straight to heaven as martyrs. Yet the people who tell them these things have not been to heaven.

In the mid-90s, Yigal Amir, a young Israeli Jew, assassinated the Prime Minister of Israel because he was pursuing peace with 'the others'. Amir was motivated to do this by religious teachers who said that it is okay to kill one who is going against their doctrine.

In both instances religion, or misinterpretation of religion, condones murder. Their logic escapes me.

The young men involved are not the chief culprits. Hypocritical interpretations of scripture were apparently fed into their minds. Neither the murderers nor those who instigated these deeds had a clear understanding of spirituality.

Religion has also condoned inhuman actions on a large scale. The Crusades, the Inquisitions in Europe and the social acceptance of slavery are examples of religious teachings condoning immoral actions.

It is important to remember that instructions or information in a scripture may be wrong, because of changes in time and place. The essence of a spiritual scripture is that it attempts to guide us toward liberation, by giving us proper instructions. These instructions may be for spiritual development or for worldly welfare. As spiritual truth is absolute, these instructions do not change over time. However, social laws may change, depending on time and place. For example, today it is generally accepted that people are monogamous. Various scriptures support this attitude. However, if there is an extreme imbalance in the male and female populations, perhaps due to war or famine, then it may be acceptable, even necessary, for women or men to have multiple partners.

So, we must be aware of the differences between spiritual instructions and social instructions in any scripture. The former, if they are rational and based on the principles of Yama and Niyama, are not changing. The latter may change from time to time.

5) *Iishvara Pranidhana*:    Iishvara means 'the controller of the universe.' Pranidhana is to 'understand clearly or adopt something as a shelter.' Iishvara Pranidhana means to establish oneself in the Cosmic Idea.

Along the way to feeling that we are living this Cosmic Ideal, we may have to fulfill many sorts of 'identity' in our lives. One man may be a father, a son, a husband, a brother, an employee, a taxpayer, etc. Though these are all true reflections of him, they are only partial reflections.

This man also has some less tangible self-perceptions. He may see himself as honest, reliable, a bit selfish, absent-minded, too talkative, loyal, intelligent, moral, a heavy drinker.

All of these reflections give him some information on how to live, on what to do; that is, these many facets of himself 'inform' him of how to act in various situations. However, the information these reflections provide is not always integrated or complete. So his self-image is incomplete.

Though we need these self-images, we also need some more general perspective. If we have a very broad view of who we are, we can whether all changes in life.

The Greek philosopher Epictetus was once beaten by his king because of a disagreement. The beating left him lame in one leg. Some time later he met a friend who said: "Oh I see you are lame now." He answered: "My leg is lame, I am not lame."

The question he is addressing here is: "Who am I?" The late Indian yogi, Ramana Maharshi, gave his students an exercise to repeat: "I am not this body, I am not this mind. I am more than this body, I am more than this mind." This exercise may be a good start to help us find out who we are.

The essence of human nature, of life itself, can be summed up in one sentence. "I am God." The essence of yoga is to help us accelerate our speed toward this realization. It is not likely that we can understand or feel or realize this essence, though, if we are constantly sheltering ourselves, covering ourselves, with a smaller image of who we are.

Iishvara Pranidhana means to take the shelter of God as our self-image. The essence of God, though, has no physicality. It is true that everything is a reflection of God. Indeed, for this reason we practice Brahmacharya and try to see the reflection of God in everything, and so to treat everything of this universe according to its spiritual value.

However, the center of God, which is our own essence, has no physical existence. So to realize God, and its value, we need to evaluate or measure God with our feelings, since no other sense we have is subtle enough to measure or contact this entity. Meditation is a tool we use to measure this entity.

## Fifteen Shiilas

Yama and Niyama stress that personal responsibility and mental clarity are important for a spiritual seeker.

Often I discuss the details of meditation with someone just coming to the practice. And it's not unusual for someone in this situation to assume that meditation will soon help their mind to become quiet and still. They are often surprised to find that many thoughts still come up in their mind. They may even feel that the mind is being flooded with more thoughts then they had before starting meditation.

Sometimes I have days on end where my meditation fills me with many blissful thoughts. I also have days where I feel much anguish and confusion. And while I have no confusion about the benefits of meditation, meditation will eventually dredge up everything in my conscience, in my memory, in my experience.

Proper meditation, especially when I use the second lesson of our meditation course, helps me surrender all my negativity and attachments.

Meditation, though, is not just internal and private. Whatever stays in my mind I will eventually express in my social life. Yama-Niyama gives me guidance on how to live my life, how to relate to others, how to determine what is right and wrong. This classic system of Yama and Niyama is, of course, very general. Anandamurti has developed another set of guidelines that are more specific. He calls these guidelines the *Fifteen Shiilas*. Shiila is a Sanskrit word which means shield. If we follow these guidelines we shield ourselves from small passions, muddy thinking and negativity in general.

In chapter one, I talked about interdependence. Humans are social beings, community beings. What we do affects others just as we are affected by what others do.

The fifteen shiilas give us a handle on what we can actually do to have a positive impact on our own thoughts and actions. Perhaps we can look at them as the practical application of Yama and Niyama.

1. *Forgiveness*:
Mahatma Gandhi said: "The weak can never forgive. Forgiveness is the attribute of the strong." It is also an attribute of the wise.

The purpose of forgiveness is to show that a problem has been resolved. It is illogical and dangerous to forgive someone who has not corrected his or her bad actions. It is, of course, important that we have guidelines in society to determine what behavior is acceptable. Yama and Niyama are the most comprehensive base for this determination.

We should not forgive someone for their irresponsible or harmful conduct until we have some sense they are correcting it. And to help a person to do this we may need to help him to correct his weaknesses. As well, if we forgive someone just because they mouthed some words of apology, they may then start to think that mere words can solve problems.

Frances Vaughan and Roger Walsh write that forgiveness is a statement or a wish that we not be separated from our human family, no matter what they've done in the past.

2. *Magnanimity of mind*:
This means to have a real concern for the welfare of others, whether in social or individual circumstances. Magnanimity of mind comes through actions, more than through words. While it may be useful to console a sick friend, for example, it may be far more beneficial to offer them some practical help in their time of need.

In the larger society, magnanimity means to understand and respect each other's views. Every country contains people from different ethnic origins, religions, races, languages, etc., and if we have no magnanimity toward others we head toward social disintegration. A garden with only one type of flower of one color and fragrance has less beauty, richness and vitality than a garden of many flowers and plants..

3. *Perpetual restraint of behavior and temper*:
Competitive athletes have one trick that sometimes helps them to gain an advantage over their opponents. Get the opponent to lose his temper. When he loses his temper, he loses control. He is off balance.

Just as an athlete needs mental balance, so do we in our daily life. If we can follow santosha, a part of Yama and Niyama, which we discussed above, then we can have perpetual restraint. We don't need to make our temper disappear. It's enough that we control it.

'Restraint' is not repression. There may be times when you must express your temper, for example, when a child is misbehaving, and you may need to show some anger. However, you should express your anger just for a short time. Then let the child know that you love him, so that your anger doesn't pull you apart from him.

4. *Readiness to sacrifice everything of the individual life for the ideology.*

In common parlance we think of an ideology as any sort of political, social or economic belief or viewpoint. Thus, we might talk about a conservative ideology or a particular economic ideology.

In Tantra, ideology is the conception of *idea*. Idea, as used here, refers to spiritual truth. There is one spiritual truth for everyone. In our daily life, we may find that different attitudes or lifestyles are relevant for different people since after all, we all live in such different circumstances from each other. And what is true in the world is only relative. One might be rich with £1,000 in the bank in a poor country. In a wealthier country, that same amount of money may just be subsistence.

Spiritual truth (which I here call idea) though, doesn't ever change. If we want the fullness of perfect peace or happiness we take a certain practice or path. If the practice is comprehensive it will work for me in the early 21st century and for anyone else anywhere, anytime.

So, we have an ideology when we are trying to connect our own thoughts and consciousness with the universal consciousness. That is, ideology is the practical expression or use of idea.

Ideology also means to follow an ideal in one's life.

In another sense, the word means 'mirror.' A mirror helps me observe my outer self, while ideology helps me observe my inner self. It gives me guidelines and methods (such as Yama and Niyama) to develop my full capacity. If I'm honest with myself, this mirror shows me who I really am now.

We can have true peace in this world only if our life is guided by inner spiritual inspiration.

If we follow Yama and Niyama then our spiritual life will naturally help us develop more compassion for all beings. Thus, it will become natural for us to sacrifice small private pleasures to help others reach a state of perfect peace.

5. *All round self-restraint*:
We can achieve little in life if we can't control our emotions and our mind. In Tantra, restraint doesn't mean to hold back, to repress or keep down. It means to guide or channel our various propensities so we can use our strengths properly and improve our weak points.

Until I learned meditation, I had little control over my mind. Fear might hold me one minute, soon to be overtaken by the urge for junk food, or sleeping all day, or one or another of many desires. Though I could understand that these desires did not help me find happiness, I had not the mental strength to look for anything more useful in my life. I started to gain the needed mental strength when I took up the regular practice of meditation.

We all know the popular saying: "The spirit is strong but the flesh is weak." This is used to rationalize our desires for drinking, overeating or any other 'desire' that we feel we shouldn't really desire. Some pundits modify this phrase to express the real situation: "The spirit is weak, but the flesh is strong."

Through diet, yogic exercises, fasting and other techniques we can guide the sensual desires to a more spiritual path, so that we use them, rather than being controlled by them.

Meditation is an essential tool to help us develop self-restraint. Proper diet and exercise are also important tools for developing self-restraint. They will do little, though, to bring our senses and emotions under control without proper guidance from the mind.

*6. Sweet and smiling behavior:*
A couple of years ago while visiting a new city, I went to shop in an upscale natural foods store. At the checkout counter the cashier was exceptionally friendly and courteous, but something in his demeanor left me with an uncomfortable feeling. I soon realized that while his words were quite friendly, he didn't really look at me, nor try to engage me in the conversation. He was talking to me because he was trained to do that, though I had no feeling that he was really interested in me.

On the other hand, one friend of mine is very straightforward and honest with his feelings. He often has good, constructive observations about people. However, he often expresses his observations in a loud voice, with anger or criticism. Most people, including me, have trouble accepting what he says simply because of his style. If he were more cordial, he would find many hearts and minds open to his viewpoint.

*7. Moral courage:*
Chogyam Trungpa said: "The essence of human bravery is refusing to give up on anyone or anything." Wendell Phillips noted that: "Physical bravery is an animal instinct; moral bravery is a much higher and truer courage." Anandamurti notes that simplicity, straightforwardness and moral courage combine to help us reach noble goals.

Moral courage is a personal trait in the service of others. And while a person exhibiting moral courage may need to retreat sometimes, they won't give up until they complete their responsibilities.

So, as well as being personal and selfless, moral courage also requires persistence and sacrifice. When we read about the feats of a hero, we may not be able to share the inner struggles that they go through to overcome difficulties. This silent, unknown, unsung persistence is sometimes the most courageous part of heroism.

8. *Setting an example by individual conduct before asking anybody to do the same.*

This attitude gives strength to our words and actions, thus helping us to develop a strong character. No matter how often I tell you not to smoke or drink (for example), can I convince you to stop the habit if I drink or smoke?

Our example needs to be more than 'what not to do.' The father of two of my best friends in childhood was an alcoholic. Though the father warned them against drinking, his own example didn't help, and while the older brother learned not to drink, because of his father's destructive behavior, his younger brother was fascinated, and ultimately seriously injured, by adopting his father's habit of drinking.

Even if we try to set a positive example by actions and words, our attitude is also important. We can set an example more through humility than through piety or pride. A teetotaler is not always good at convincing us to stay sober. Is he a prim, fussy man who always speaks in platitudes and spends all Sabbath praying, probably boring God as much as he bores us? If so, I don't think his words or example will inspire us.

9. *Keeping oneself aloof from criticizing others, condemning others, mudslinging and all sorts of groupism.*

This point naturally follows the shiilas we've discussed so far. My words and actions can have no moral force if I am criticizing or gossiping all the time. I may be very intelligent, in a way, and I may be physically strong. However, my willpower will become less and my actions and thoughts less effective if I spend much of my time condemning and criticizing others.

Politicians are well known for criticizing and mudslinging. It seems that it's easier to criticize than to develop good policies.

Stephen Covey identifies people of this nature as 'reactive,' meaning that they don't take responsibility for their actions. If they lose in life, they blame others. Anandamurti notes that such people are usually motivated by a fear complex.

A person who can anticipate a situation, and is ready, willing and able to respond is a 'responsible' person, who, by definition is busy making the best of any situation. A reactive person may take care of his basic obligations. However he has not developed the inner strength, the moral courage, to overcome all diffi-culties, to turn them to his advantage. Naturally it's easier for this type of person to criticize and condemn others, instead of taking responsibility for his weaknesses. Weaknesses can always be overcome if we face them and understand them.

There is a story about a respected Rabbi who had a stutter. In one town, he had just finished a public talk. One man came up to him who disagreed with the Rabbi. He started abusing the Rabbi, calling him all sorts of names. The Rabbi remained quiet during this time. He then said to the man: "And you sir, are a stutterer." The man eyed the Rabbi carefully, as if the Rabbi had become disoriented. "Excuse me, Rabbi, but you have a stutter, I don't." "Yes," said the Rabbi. "That is true. But you were just offering me all of your bad qualities, so I thought I would offer you mine."

Look close at those you know who criticize and condemn others. I often find that what I criticize in another person reflects something in me. If I really care about the other person, I should help him or her overcome whatever problems I see in them.

10. *Strict adherence to the principles of Yama and Niyama.*
Yama and Niyama are not only guidelines to carry us to a better life, but also shields against misfortune. Everyone has difficulties in life. The more spiritual evolution or intellectual maturity you have, the more problems or challenges you may have. As you become more mature, you can handle more challenges.

A baby has very few problems or challenges. It has little capability to do much in life. The president of a country has many more problems and challenges, thus many more opportu-nities, compared to the young child. It may seem illogical in a way. After all, since the president has so much power at his or her disposal, can't they just use their power to avoid problems? Just the opposite: problems or challenges come to those who can handle them.

Anandamurti says, "Difficulties will never be greater than our capacity to solve them." In this viewpoint, Yama and Niyama are great aids to solving any problem. They keep balance, harmony and determination in the forefront of our life.

Difficulty, of course, is not the same for everyone. One person, when given the duty to, say, negotiate the release of hostages from a hijacked airplane, may feel that it is a very difficult task. Another person, when given the same task, may see it as a great opportunity to save the lives of innocent people.

Yama and Niyama help each of us to have an integrated personality and thus take a positive view of life.

11. *Due to carelessness, if any mistake is committed unknowingly or unconsciously, one must admit it immediately and ask for punishment.* This point shields us against accumulating mental distortions. Many of the mistakes I make are probably due to carelessness, though this doesn't mean that I'm unaware that I made a mistake. When I do realize I made a mistake I have two choices: I can avoid responsibility or take responsibility. If I avoid responsibility I may directly or indirectly be shifting the blame to someone else.

If I avoid taking responsibility I am breaking the guidelines of asteya and ahimsa. I will certainly have trouble maintaining mental balance, or santosha. When I avoid admitting my mistakes fear finds a niche in my mind. Gradually it starts to take over a larger part of my mind, just as bacteria multiply in a conducive environment.

I can't avoid blame for my original mistake. It's compounded if someone sees that I am also a liar, so it's better to admit the mistake now and get it over with. Asking for punishment is for my benefit, not so much for the benefit of those I've wronged. This request on my part will clear my mind of any lingering guilt for my mistake.

12. *Even while dealing with a person of inimical nature, one must keep oneself free from hatred, anger and vanity.*

One story about Gautama the Buddha illustrates this point. After his realization, he spent many years traversing India to teach the people what he learned. After one talk, a man came up to him and started criticizing him strongly. Perhaps it was an ancestor of the man who had criticized the Rabbi, whom I mentioned earlier.

The Buddha was silent. The man continued his abuse and Buddha continued his silence. After some time the man asked Buddha if he didn't have any response to him. The Buddha remained silent till the man was finished. The man was perplexed that Buddha didn't argue with him, didn't challenge him. The Buddha, understanding his perplexity, said: "If I'd responded to you then it would have been, in a sense, accepting your criticism and abuse. If you offer me a gift, it remains yours until I accept it. It is the same with your words. Until I accept what you say, it still belongs to you."

Silence is one way to distance yourself from negativity or hostility. At other times it may be appropriate to argue a valid point. However, if you argue with hostile, inimical people you are, in a sense, accepting their bad nature and perhaps encouraging them to continue in this way.

It may be easy to feel hatred or anger toward an obnoxious person. Hatred, anger and vanity are short-term responses that may satisfy us because of our own psychological immaturity. The most productive way to deal with inimical people, I think, is to go one step further than Buddha did in the story. Of course I don't want to receive anyone's negativity. As well, I don't want them to hold onto it. So I can try to help them replace it by projecting positive qualities, qualities opposite to theirs.

If you hate a person, or are angry with him or her, you are

encouraging your own lower nature. It will be difficult if not impossible to inspire the other to give up similar qualities. We must also be careful of vanity, such as an attitude that, "I'm so much more sensible and polite than she is." Your vanity cannot motivate you to help another person remove their inimical nature.

13. *One should keep aloof from talkativeness.*
If I find someone who talks excessively, I can often feel that they have some tension or loneliness inside that they can't work out.

Sometimes people talk too much because they don't want to confront what's in their mind. Talking is good for covering up issues we may not want to deal with. It may also cover up loneliness.

To keep aloof from talkativeness is a shield for a few reasons. It helps us see the larger world outside of our own sphere. Silence encourages us to learn. George Eliot lauds the person who, "having nothing to say, abstains from giving wordy evidence of the fact."

There is a yogic saying that we should think a thousand times before talking. This may not always be practical, but the spirit of the idea is that less talking is a way of controlling the mind. Thus, if I check my habit of too much talking I can listen more, learn more and appreciate the world and my fellow humans more. All of this can help me control vanity and become wiser.

14. *Obedience to a structural code of discipline.*
Structure, "something arranged in a definite pattern of organization" is essential for our lives. The most basic structure that each of us has, that we deal with constantly, is the body and mind. Whenever either one is 'de-structured' or disoriented, we suffer. One important aspect of yoga is to develop self-control, that is, to develop discipline.

If I let my mind and body run wherever they want I may end

up with a lot of temporary happiness, but pain will soon follow. A code of discipline helps me to distinguish short-term happiness from long-term happiness.

So, the self-control of a structural code of discipline helps me to integrate my life and to learn what my possibilities in life are. In fact, if my structural code is comprehensive, I learn to increase my possibilities in life.

In yoga I learn to examine my personal weaknesses. If they are negative weaknesses I can learn to channel them out of existence. A 'positive' weakness is a trait that is good, but just has not been developed. For example, I may want to increase my aptitude or inclination to study. Yoga can help me develop my mental strength so I can study more.

A structural code is like a base in life. Everyone needs some sort of base. It may be your work, your family or your studies; it may be some character or personality trait you have that enables you to do what you need to do. Self-control, discipline, will help us be successful in our chosen life's work.

15. *Sense of responsibility.*
The ability to respond to a situation is a positive, productive ability. When we react to a situation, we can't have control over it.

Imagine yourself as a teacher who has a pupil who is always morose, uncooperative and withdrawn. A little forethought and experience will help you understand that he may eventually cause trouble for you or himself. If you have the ability to respond to him and his situation, you can take steps to help him find a positive direction in his life.

A sense of responsibility is positive, constructive and requires some forethought, to try to understand or predict what may happen at any time, in a given situation.

"The willingness to accept responsibility for one's own life is the source from which self-respect springs", said Joan Didion.

## Chapter 5

# SPIRITUAL PRACTICES: THE WAY TO GET THERE

"It is this belief in a power larger than myself and other than myself which allows me to venture into the unknown and even the unknowable."
— Maya Angelou

"We know what we are, but know not what we may be."
— William Shakespeare

"Your treasure house is within; it contains all you'll ever need."
— Hui-Hai

Having just returned back to my university to start my second year I soon ran into Caylor, a friend of mine from our first year. I had spent much of my summer working in a gas station and, incidentally, soaking up the news about the first man landing on the moon. Caylor, in contrast, had gone to the Woodstock music festival, which in the long view was perhaps not as significant as landing on the moon; however, Woodstock probably had more direct or immediate impact than the moon landing on the lives of a lot of people.

Caylor had also learned, that summer, something else that would have a longer lasting impact on his life, and also on mine.

He had learned about something called yoga. I guess I'd heard the term. I remembered that when I was in high school I'd heard that the Beatles had met someone named Maharishi from India and learned something called yoga; that was as much as I could remember about yoga.

That afternoon, Caylor shared his experiences of the summer, particularly about this new found thing called yoga. He discussed his understanding of it and showed me some exercises (some that were impossible for me to do and others that I seemed able to do naturally). And then he noted that besides these strange but calming exercises, there was a central practice of yoga called meditation.

This was a lot more fascinating to me than the yoga exercises. As weeks went by I learned from him about the mystical traditions of India and that the human mind, the human experience, is potentially much more than we can normally imagine. A few books made their way into my hands, from his bookshelves. These books, such as *Autobiography of a Yogi* by Yogananda, and *The Master Game*, by Robert De Ropp, opened me to a world that I previously could hardly have imagined.

I continued to explore yoga (particularly the meditation aspect, which is the essential part of yogic discipline) by reading books, going to lectures and classes and trying in my own way to do some type of meditation. At that point I was not ready for the 'real thing', and I saw friend after friend taking up one or another meditation or spiritual practice. However I was just not settled for it yet. I could talk about meditation and yoga, and I felt I had more understanding than many others who were actually doing it. (Such type of knowledge is hard to prove, and eventually I realized that yogic practice without a great deal of yogic knowledge is more useful than knowledge without experience.)

Eventually I wanted the real, the deeper, the personal knowledge and experience of meditation so much that I was able to lay aside my reservations and self-doubts enough to take up the practice. I've never looked back.

Why did I eventually take up the practice, rather than to continue just reading the books? I guess I finally understood that meditation can take a person far beyond the confusions of our worldly life, without having to leave the world.

We practice meditation in order to, ultimately, find perfect peace or happiness. The source of happiness is inside us. This inner peace does not mean we will have no difficulties. It does, however, give us the clarity of mind to solve difficulties when they do come along.

Peace of mind is essentially the same as happiness. Happiness is a state of mental composure. It can come from seeing your football team win a game, from gaining high marks in school, from your lover or from a glass of beer (or two or three).

However, these types of happiness are generally short lived and depend on something outside of you.

The yogi and the pleasure seeker both want happiness; both want mental peace or equanimity. They both want to feel good about themselves. So what is the difference?

A pleasure seeker, a hedonist, might say he wants the same thing as a yogi: happiness. However, the pleasures of a playboy are temporary. When a pleasure ends the playboy doesn't look for deeper, more lasting happiness. He looks for the same thing again, though perhaps in a different form, or in greater quantity.

My experience as a meditation teacher shows me that if a hedonist would have a change of heart and start to seek spiritual secrets, he may have trouble practicing meditation even if he accepts that it is a valuable and valid pursuit. This is because he associates happiness with certain sensations. He has come to think happiness must follow from certain actions or rituals that he's used to. He associates happiness with superficial or immediate physical and mental stimuli and may well receive support for his lifestyle from his friends.

To change his lifestyle, the pleasure seeker may have to 're-program' his nervous system, which so far has learned to derive happiness from quick, temporary, sensual pleasure. He may not have the patience or strength of mind to immediately start the long journey leading to spiritual fulfillment. If our hedonist decides to pursue meditation, he may have to go through a considerable period of inner cleansing, a cleansing — both mental and physical -- which is necessary if he wants to make a radical change in his thinking habits.

Even if you are not a hedonist, you may have some difficulty in pursuing meditation. For most of us meditation is a new habit to add to our daily life. While the practice of meditation may not be difficult, finding time in our daily schedule to do it may take some effort. The positive reinforcement we expect from meditation may also not be so obvious every time we sit for meditation. It will probably not be a feedback directly from the senses. Thus we may have to let the mind become quieter than usual before we can become aware of the benefits of meditation.

If you do not have at least some control of your mind, this lack of control, as I noted, can make it difficult to practice meditation. Many people who attend my classes have, I would say, a decent amount of control over their lives, whether they are students or professionals. They are able to fulfill their responsibilities; they may well have very good marks in school, and good memories. However, the self-control that one needs to practice meditation regularly is not always there. Constant effort, or self-discipline is of course important for regular meditation practice, and a teacher is also very important. A teacher can often see your weaknesses easier than you can and can then provide guidance as to how to overcome them.

To be aware of your weaknesses is an important first step. Then you need to make an effort to overcome the weaknesses. Otherwise they will continue to dominate your mind; in one or another way, mental weaknesses also limit your experience of the world. Mental weaknesses also reduce the clarity with which you see the world, as the fog of emotion blocks your vision.

We can clear away this fog with the regular practice of meditation and other yogic practices.

The Ananda Marga system of meditation offers a standard

course of six lessons. They are similar to the Astaunga Yoga system of Patanjali. The lessons help us to do such things as refine our mind, increase our concentration or purify our mental or physical body. The first five lessons are a preparation for the sixth lesson, properly called meditation, or *dhyana*. It is an experience you should not miss if you want to expand your mental and spiritual borders.

These lessons are always taught to students personally and privately. The specifics of each lesson are not to be shared with anyone, and should only be discussed between the student and the teacher.

In this following section I will give a general description of the lessons simply to show a broad overview of the purpose of each lesson.

**First Lesson:**
Imagine a small river, flowing along its fixed course, day-by-day, year-by-year. The river is home to numerous fish and other sea life. It welcomes boats, swimmers and rainfall. It may give some of itself to power a hydroelectric plant or to irrigate a farmer's fields.

Yes, the river has some use. It has some power. However, its significance pales in comparison to an ocean. When this river water enters the ocean, it becomes part of a greater organism, spanning the globe and expressing the full power and majesty of a body of water. In a sense, when the river merges into the ocean it has reached its destination.

Now imagine a drop of milk. Compare this to a pot of milk. If you examine their chemical properties, you will see that both the drop and pot of milk are the same. The taste of both is also the same. The essential difference is that you can do very little with a drop of milk. If you put it on your tongue you may taste it for a brief moment, but then it's gone, leaving you as thirsty as before.

You can drink from a pot of milk to your heart's content. You can also make yogurt, buttermilk or butter from a pot of milk. You can use it in a cake or bread mix. The drop of milk has all the characteristics of the milk in the pot. It has, however, very little capacity compared to the pot of milk. But when the drop enters the pot of milk it can do everything the milk in the pot can do. It has become part of a greater whole. It has, so to speak, reached its destination.

The human being is, in a sense, like the river or the drop of milk. We have the capacity to do much more in our lives than we normally do. We can lead a more fulfilling, productive life if we can tap into our greater self, our higher identity.

Tantra refers to this higher identity as self-knowledge. A yogic saying notes that self-knowledge is the only true knowledge and that all other knowledge is a shadow of self-knowledge. A narrow view of this attitude has lead some people to live a solitary life, pretty much giving up on the world, and giving up on exploring the world and learning new things about the world. This is a passive attitude that Tantra would not support. However, Tantra is known as a 'middle path' because it supports worldly or material progress but not at the cost of losing our spiritual base. Rather Tantric teachers propose that we should use science and other sorts of knowledge to make our lives more fulfilling. This happens when we develop things that give us more time and health so that we can pursue subtle things such as the arts, being in nature and ultimately, spiritual pursuits.

So we need to live on many levels, trying to be careful not to, as the Beatle's sung, 'gain the world and lose our soul'. I think that finding a balance of enjoying the world but not forgetting our ultimate goal is one of our most difficult tasks.

You can certainly forget about the stresses of life by taking a couple of drinks, or taking one or another drugs. And many people do this. People I meet tell me that this helps them to go into some other frame of mind that relaxes them. Is this not a way of finding peace, I'm sometimes asked.

Well, no, it isn't. For its effects are very temporary and tend to attract you back more and more to that type of release, whether it is drinking, drugging, smoking or something else. I daresay that these things don't let go of you easily and don't give you any permanent way to feel and act really free. For you may be a bit free of the stress and worries of life, but it's only for the moment and is dependent on just another 'thing' out there (tobacco or alcohol, or whatever else) that won't let go of you, or won't let you let go of it.

The true self of each of us is the same as the Cosmic Mind. There is something within each of us which is permanent and which reflects our higher self. Every part of the human body will eventually die. But there is something in each of us that can give us ultimate security. We can experience this security if we can identify this higher self. Almost everyone spends their time, day in and day out, preoccupied with their limited self, and while it is important to take care of every aspect of our life, it seems to me we often forget our true identity.

The Cosmic Mind cannot be sensed as we can sense things of the world. We cannot taste, smell, touch, see or hear this part of our self. This essential part of our self can only be realized as a mental feeling.

The lessons of Ananda Marga meditation are a process to help us identify our individual self with our complete or Supreme Self. The foundation for this process is the *first lesson*. This lesson centers on the recitation of an *ishta mantra*. A mantra is a sound, or a combination of sounds. In Tantra yogic practices, we always repeat an ishta mantra in the mind, never with the voice.

One question I often receive in this regard is: "You mean all I need to do is close my eyes and repeat this word?" Well, no, not quite. For one thing, as I explained above, a mantra is not just a word.

Tantric theory views sound as the first vibration created in the universe. Anandamurti writes that: "Everything in this manifest universe is vibrational. Creation is also vibrational. And the first and subtlest expression of the vibrational flow is (sound)."

Mantra means "that collection of sounds, meditation on which leads to liberation" Not every sound can qualify as a mantra. Take this simple example of the need to have the right sound, or word, in the right situation. Imagine that you are sitting somewhere and have not the strength to get up and walk. A man walks by you and you say to him: "Come, sir, let's have a little talk." Well, he may end up talking with you, but he will not necessarily help you to get up from your seat. You need to use the right words to achieve that result, by saying something like: "Sir, I've not the strength to walk. Can you help me?"

Thus with a mantra, the correct sound needs to be used to become a mantra. In sum: "when a particular feeling is expressed through a particular combination of sounds, it achieves a particular value."

A proper mantra is vibrating simultaneously in the Cosmos and in the individual person. The most profound use of a mantra, then, is to help a person to bring their personal flow or vibration in harmony with the universal flow.

There are many uses or benefits from mantra meditation. In the early stages of meditation, there are some 'ground level' benefits. These include giving the user more relaxation, concentration or peace of mind. However, at higher levels of meditation, a mantra is, according to Anandamurti: "That which, when contemplated on, leads to freedom from (all sorts of) bondages."

Lama Anagarika Govinda says a proper mantra can never mislead us. Rather, it seeks "the dissolution of impediments, the loosening of knots into which we have entangled ourselves consciously and unconsciously by our desires, prejudices, and the accumulated effects of our attachments."

Ishta means 'spiritual goal' or 'terminus.' Thus, an ishta

mantra is a tool we use to help us reach our highest goal.

An ishta mantra has three primary qualities. First, it is pulsative or rhythmic. An ishta mantra always has two syllables. Thus you can repeat it in rhythm with your breathing. You repeat the first syllable with every inhalation and the second with every exhalation. This cadence makes it easier to repeat the mantra. Meditation in this manner helps the mind to obtain a deeper state of awareness.

Secondly, the ishta mantra has a personal relationship to you. Each of us has our own nature, our own personal vibration or rhythm. The universe also has a rhythm, which is a combination of all the individual rhythms. When we are able to harmonize ourselves with the universal rhythm we gain fulfillment. The proper mantra, as noted above, is one that helps your mind to attune itself to the universal rhythm.

Many years ago yogis discovered that different sounds attract certain types of people. We may draw an analogy to music, since people are attracted to different types of music. The attraction music holds for us has little to do with the musical ability of the listeners. My musical talent ends at putting on a CD and adjusting the volume. Yet I can enjoy and appreciate good music.

You do not receive the ishta mantra because of the spiritual elevation you have already attained; rather, it is a vehicle to increase your speed on the road to spiritual elevation.

The third quality of an ishta mantra is its meaning. Some schools of yoga assign mantras that are mere sounds to repeat, for which the meditator does not know the meaning. This method may help you to relax. However, relaxation is a minor goal of meditation. An ishta mantra, by its definition, directs our attention towards our Supreme Self, and to be able to do this we need to know its meaning.

Swami Prabhavananda notes that every word has its own mental climate. Repeat a word such as 'war' or 'money' or 'useless' over and over. Your mood will be influenced by the associations these words have for you.

An Ista Mantra of course has a positive, universal meaning. So its repetition, with an understanding of the meaning, will create the mental climate inherent in the idea of the mantra.

When we properly use a mantra that has these three qualities, each of us is gradually able to "Know thyself." The mantra is, in a sense, a seed of spiritual realization. As the seed of a tree contains all that is needed to make a tree sprout forth, so a mantra contains the power to help our true spiritual nature sprout forth. Of course the mantra, like the seedling of the tree, needs a proper environment to be able to grow.

A mantra receives its power from a 'mental energizing process.' In the chapter on the *Guru* we will discuss this process.

I want to make a short comment on some of the terminology. The yogic word for meditation is *dhyana*. This means a 'flowing of the mind.' If you have at all practiced meditation you can understand that it is not easy to enter this state of mind. The section below on the sixth lesson of our meditation course describes what this 'flowing of the mind' is. Our first five lessons, while very valuable in themselves, are, in a sense, preparation for actual meditation. It is important to distinguish between the preparatory stages and meditation itself. Thus we use another word to describe these lessons. The word is *sadhana*. It means 'concentrated effort' or 'effort to make oneself complete.'

---

**Thoughts and Water:**

The meaning we associate with a word seems to have an effect on our mind, on our attitudes and on our motivations. This seems true in humans and some significant experiments apparently show that our thoughts can influence the shape of water crystals.

The website, http://www.whatthebleep.com/crystals/

---

des-cribes some unusual experiments:

Dr. Masaru Emoto, from Japan, seems to have shown that thoughts and feelings affect physical reality. By producing different focused intentions through written and spoken words and music and literally presenting it to the same water samples, the water appears to "change its expression".

Essentially, Dr. Emoto captured water's 'expressions.' He developed a technique using a very powerful microscope in a very cold room along with high-speed photography, to photograph newly formed crystals of frozen water samples. Not all water samples crystallize however. Water samples from extremely polluted rivers directly seem to express the 'state' the water is in.

Dr. Emoto discovered that crystals formed in frozen water reveal changes when specific, concentrated thoughts are directed toward them. He found that water from clear springs and water that has been exposed to loving words shows brilliant, complex, and colorful snowflake patterns. In contrast, polluted water, or water exposed to negative thoughts, forms incomplete, asymmetrical patterns with dull colors.

## Second Lesson:

The second lesson is a method to help us see the essential consciousness and unity in everything and in every action. Our ideation in the first lesson is to see that the source of our existence is God, or the supreme consciousness. Second lesson helps us to see this consciousness as the base or essence of everything, every-where, all the time.

The main purpose of the second lesson is to remind us that everything is God. Yes, an ant you step on is God, the food you eat is God, your action of taking a bath or turning on the radio is God.

When we see everything in this light then we can give proper value to everything. If you are, for example, a doctor, the practice of second lesson can remind you to take extra care of the many forms of God-consciousness who come to you office. A murderer or thief who took up this practice of second lesson could not easily continue their 'occupation.' Why? Certain actions harm others (and ultimately ourselves). If I know we are all part of one consciousness, that we all come from the same source, then I know that when I harm others I am, ultimately, harming myself.

A shopkeeper who practices second lesson will treat his or her customers with respect and never cheat them. Of course this does not happen just as a result of simply following a formula learned from your meditation teacher. We need to understand the idea behind the second lesson. This is also true for the first lesson.

Concerning second lesson, we may see the world from one of two perspectives. We may see that everyone is different from everyone else. Or we can see we all have some essential unifying qualities. This latter view is the basis for Brahmacharya, the fourth principle of the yogic moral code, Yama.

Both these views have some truth to them. It's very easy to see things from the perspective of difference. On the surface it is obvious that we are all different.

George Leonard says, "At the heart of each of us, whatever our imperfections, there exists a silent pulse of perfect rhythm... which is absolutely individual and unique and yet which connects us to everything in the universe."

I might add that while the concept of Brahmacharya has been around since ancient times, Anandamurti is the first guru to create a technique to awaken this consciousness.

The rational foundation for the second lesson is that according to Tantra philosophy there are three basic differences between the objects of the world. *First*, there are different types or species of objects. A human is different from a dog, a tree or a fish. *Secondly*, within every species there are differences. Trees may be elms, maples, palms, etc. And of course each tree is different from every other tree. Every human is also unique, and there are various ethnic, linguistic and other strains within the human family. *Thirdly*, within one entity there are differences. A tree has leaves, roots, bark, etc. A human has arms, legs, a brain, a heart, etc.

None of these differences suggest superiority or inferiority. Rather, they suggest that each part and each being has a purpose and a value.

Life and the world take on a deeper meaning for us when we see every action and object as spiritual and purposeful. The way we look at life is, of course, all a matter of perspective. Our second lesson helps us to expand our perspective, and thus, our sense of belonging. "The universe is duly in order, everything in its place," noted Walt Whitman.

*Action and Reaction*

If we are able to practice the second lesson perfectly, every impression that enters our mind will appear as a form of God. However, whether or not we practice second lesson, everything that enters our mind will leave some impression in our memory, whether we consciously remember it or not. Yoga psychology says that every impression that enters our mind must be expressed in some form, at some time. Physical science supports this view with the idea that for every action there is an opposite reaction.

In an ideal state the human mind is pure and clear. After attaining this state, every action is done in the best way, creating no reaction.

However we all have some impressions in our mind that to some degree confuse or distort reality. Thus, we do not always act and respond in the most appropriate way. If we look at a cushion we can see an analogy of the human mind. Before anyone has touched it, the cushion may be perfectly round. As soon as you touch it, you leave an impression in the cushion. After some moments the impression leaves the cushion, which then returns to its normal shape. If you place a bottle of water on the cushion, it leaves an impression as long as the bottle is there. Even after you remove the bottle, the impression will still be there for some time. The amount of time the impression stays depends on the weight of the bottle and how long it remained on the cushion.

The human mind is always taking in impressions, or information, or 'data.' If we file this data in the right place we can respond to it in the best way at the best time. If your mind is disorganized however, your response will also lack perfect clarity.

Our present personality and character and our present actions are, of course, the result of our past actions and the impressions we have received. Thus, what we do now is either something that may cause a later reaction or is itself the result of an earlier action. We are each formed by the law of action and reaction.

In yoga, this law has two names. One is *karma*. This means 'action'. The other word is *samskara*. This is a 'reaction in potentiality', or a reaction waiting to be expressed. Each of us has a certain amount of samskaras. Though we may be able to measure one's weight, blood type or IQ, we cannot measure the samskaras of a person. For the sake of discussion, let's say you have a thousand samskaras. This means that your mind is like a cushion with a thousand impressions in it. The cushion will be in the best condition when there are no impressions. In the same way, your mind will be in balance when you have removed those thousand samskaras.

You may, however, acquire more samskaras, or impressions while trying to rid yourself of your existing samskaras.

We can avoid gaining new samskaras by practicing the second lesson. The practice of the second lesson helps us to put everything in its proper place, mentally.

According to yoga, we can only eliminate our samskaras after they have matured in the mind. Then they are ready to be expressed. Maturation occurs in one of three ways:

1. After a period of senselessness,
2. After physical death, or
3. During sadhana (meditation).

These three conditions have one striking similarity. In each state, the mind is dissociated from the body. During senselessness and sadhana, the mind is not physically separated from the body. Rather, it is unconcerned with the body. Physical death of course separates the mind and the body.

One may notice that a victim of a serious accident, after regaining consciousness, may experience a drastic change in his or her life. This is because certain samskaras have matured and are now ready to express themselves.

In terms of expressing samskaras, sadhana has at least one advantage over the other two conditions. After death or senselessness, one may exhaust old samskaras. At the same time, however, we want to express new desires. For example, you may have acquired a samskara that will get expressed when you lose your wallet. The old samskara has thus been expressed, but it may happen that your anger at the loss creates a new samskara for you.

As we go deep into our sadhana our ego can sometimes become 'inactive.' When this occurs we may become aware that some of our old habits are no longer useful to us. The practice of sadhana gives us the inner strength and clarity to let go of these impressions or habits.

Social service, in the form of tapah (the third point of Niyama), is also an important way to avoid accumulating new samskaras.

Another part of second lesson is a mental offering we make at the end of every session of sadhana. This is *Guru Puja*, which means 'an offering to the Guru.' During meditation many thoughts may come into the mind. They may include memories and emotions as well as subtle spiritual feelings. A thought or feeling that comes up in meditation can create a deep impression in our minds. At the end of meditation, we offer all the mental impressions, acquired during meditation, to the guru. This has the effect of freeing our mind from attachments which may drag us backwards or downwards, and slow us down in our search for spiritual freedom.

We also practice this part of second lesson during our collective weekly meditation, called *dharmachakra*.

During guru puja we imagine we are holding a flower, or flowers, in the palm of our hand. The color of the flowers you offer should represent a color of your mind. What color is your mind? Well, every thought or emotion has a subtle color associated with it. We try to feel which color or colors were dominant in our mind during sadhana. Then we offer this to the guru, who, spiritually, will help rid us of any unnecessary attachments we might have acquired during meditation.

The second lesson is called *Madhuvidya*. This means 'honey knowledge.' As we learn to see God consciousness in everything, we develop a sweeter feeling in our heart toward every aspect of life.

### Third Lesson:

This lesson is called *Tattva Dharana*, which means "concentration on the factors." According to Tantra, this physical universe is composed of a combination of five factors. These are: ether, air, light, liquid and solid. Twenty-first century science has not yet found a way to definitively measure or prove the existence of ether but the other four factors are obvious.

Ether, also spelled aether, does, however, have some proponents among modern scientists. Even Albert Michaelson, whose famous 1887 experiment, done with Edward Morley, was considered to be the first strong evidence against ether, said that we don't have to reject ether, just because of the relativity theory. As well as Michaelson, other physicists such as Herbert Ives, Paul Dirac and Geoffrey Builder expressed support for the possibility of ether existing.

The yogic view of these five factors is that each factor, in the order listed above, is denser than the preceding one. According to Tantra theory ether developed first. After that came air, which is denser than ether. The process continued — from lighter to heavier — until all the five factors existed. Any being, whether a rock, a bird, a glass of milk, a star or a human, is a combination of these factors. As these factors combine along with other variables, such as pressure and density, an object takes on a physical shape and function.

Humans have a physical nervous system, but they also have a psychic nervous system. Several psychic and psycho-spiritual factors go into constructing this psychic nervous system.

The basis of this psycho-spiritual system is *prana*. Prana means vital energy. We will discuss prana in more detail when we talk about the fourth lesson.

According to Tantra, prana flows through our bodies along certain psycho-spiritual channels called *nadiis*. There are three primary nadiis in the human body. Nadii means river, and in India people sometimes call these nadiis by the names of the three main rivers of India.

We will however call them by their standard names. One nadii or channel is the *Susumna*. This nadii starts, as do the other two, at the base of the spine. It is located within the spinal column and goes straight up to the brain. Another nadii, the *Ida*, starts on the left side of the Susumna. The third nadii, the *Piungala*, starts on the right side of the Susumna. The Ida and Piungala zigzag up the body. They cross each other and the Susumna, at certain points. The points where they cross are called chakras.

A *chakra*, which means circle, is a psychic nerve center. Each chakra has many qualities and character- istics associated with it. Tantric meditation uses the chakras in many ways. The accompanying diagrams show the location of the seven main chakras, and the three nadiis.

Each of the five lower chakras controls – within the individual – one of the five fundamental factors. The first chakra controls the solid factor, the second chakra to the liquid factor, and so on.

Thus when a particular chakra is healthy, the associated factor (solid, liquid, etc.) in your body is also healthy. Some asanas help to balance the chakras. For example, if you have digestive problems it often means you have a problem with the third chakra, which relates to the element of fire. Certain asanas can help to balance this chakra and therefore help solve the digestive problems. Although the chakras are invisible to the normal eye, they form a bridge between the psychic and physical aspects of our self.

Each chakra also relates to some aspects of our personality. According to Tantra, human beings possess fifty primary mental tendencies or propensities (*vrittis*). Some of these are very positive, such as spiritual longing, expression of worldly knowledge, hope, conscience, etc. Others, such as indifference, sadistic tendencies, vanity, etc., are not our best friends, and we should try to control them very well.

Asanas and proper diet are two ways to control the vrittis.

Another way is through the third meditation lesson. This lesson helps us to balance, control and strengthen each chakra. Once we have created balance or harmony in a chakra we can gradually access the mental abilities associated with that chakra. In order to maintain health, the body needs to be kept clean and to have regular exercise. This is true for both psychic and physical bodies. The third lesson of meditation is a way of exercising and thus strengthening, our chakras. The fifth lesson of meditation, which is discussed later, purifies and cleans the chakras.

There are ways of understanding if a chakra is becoming healthier. You may experience improved physical health, such as more energy, better breathing, better elimination, etc. You may also find you have more emotional control and balance. If you have a problem with shyness, for example, you may be able to overcome this problem through the practice of third lesson as well as the regular practice of the asanas your acharya prescribes for you.

It is possible to develop extra-sensory powers, such as telepathy, when you strengthen and harmonize the chakras.

Yogis in Tibet, for example, are reputed to have powers associated with the purification and strengthening of their chakras. There are many reports of Tibetan yogis who can walk or run continuously for 24 hours or more. Some yogis have been reported to cover distances on foot in a few hours that would take a normal traveler days or even weeks to cover.

Other yogic powers associated with the chakras include the capacity to generate immense body heat. Thus yogis can spend long hours in very cold areas, wearing little clothing. Some have also been known to fast for weeks, months or even years with almost no food.

Chakra balancing and strengthening can also help one to develop other mental powers. Mind reading is common among developed yogis. It is possible to know the past or future and to see non-physical beings (known as luminous bodies).

However, while these abilities and powers are fascinating, and may be useful once in awhile, Anandamurti emphasizes that they are not really relevant for spiritual growth. One or another of the occult or mental powers identified with this lesson may come to your life from time to time, but all serious and mature spiritual masters emphasize that these powers are, at best, a diversion from spiritual progress.

**Fourth Lesson:**
This lesson is called *pranayama*. *Prana*, as noted earlier, is the vital energy, or life force, within each of us. *Yama* here means observation or control. We always want to control and maintain our life force. People, however, do many things to weaken their vital energy. They may have poor diets, poor exercise routines or poor recreational habits. They may also have negative thoughts and attitudes about life. These things all cause ill health, both in the body and mind. A person suffering from ill health will not benefit from the practice of pranayama. If they want to learn pranayama they must first take steps to regain their health. It is only possible for a person in good health who is practicing the first three lessons of meditation to learn pranayama.

In this lesson prana means 'air' as well as 'vital energy.' Several languages have similar multiple meanings for this word. The English word 'inspiration' means inhalation as well as spiritual awareness. The Greek word 'pneuma' means both air and spirit. Air is of course the most essential factor for the maintenance of our life. We may go for weeks without food, for a few days without water or sleep. We may live in extreme conditions of hot or cold for a long time. With all these things we may survive. However, even a few short minutes without air will end our life.

Breathing is of course the primary way we use air. Our breathing also has a close connection to our mental state. Try running very hard for several minutes. When you stop, observe the state of your mind. Can you remember the telephone numbers you usually know? Can you recall your schedule of tasks for the day? When the breathing is very rapid, the mind tends to be in a state of agitation.

Notice yourself sometime when you are studying, in deep thought or in a calm state, perhaps listening to pleasant music. Your breathing will be very slow, regular and deep. In this state you can think, remember and understand more easily.

As our breathing affects our mind, so our mind affects our breathing. If someone is in a state of mental agitation their breathing is often rapid and shallow. They do not give their body the amount of air it requires. This lack of proper breathing can perpetuate or increase the mental agitation. Which came first, the poor breathing or the poor mental state? It depends on the particular case. However, I dare say that more often the mental state influences the quality of the breathing.

These secrets of pranayama are not new. Swami Sivapriyananda notes: "Most early civilizations, particularly those of India and China, evolved methods of controlling respiration and consequently changing the emotions and the state of consciousness."

This goes along with the findings of modern science. Excitable animals breathe more rapidly than those of a calmer nature. The hare breathes 55 times per minute, while the tortoise breathes just 3 times a minute. According to Sivapriyananda: "Yogis argue that if emotional states can affect the rate of breathing, then conversely, an alteration in the rate of respiration should alter the... emotional state."

The idea of prana is not unique to yoga or Tantra. Chinese medical science recognizes a vital force called *chi*. The flow of chi, or prana, is relevant to one's health. Acupuncture, for instance, stimulates the flow of chi in the body, thus clearing energy blockages. When the flow of the vital energy is restored, so is the patients' health. Martial arts also use breath control to center the mind and add force and balance to the performance of the practitioner.

Lama Anagarika Govinda observes that of all our vital functions, breathing is the only one we can control. Blood circulation, digestion, removal of waste, etc., are involuntary functions. We can affect their proper functioning, but we cannot control them.

Deep, regulated, sustained, controlled breathing is an instrument for connecting our individual vital energy to the universal vital energy or prana.

In the lesson of pranayama, proper breathing is even more important than in our normal routine. Pranayama is a lesson involving both controlled breathing and mental ideation. The ideation is similar to that of the first lesson. The breathing exercise of pranayama is deep, regulated and sustained. Thus the mind becomes very sensitive to what it is being 'fed.' So, before we learn pranayama we need to be practicing our meditation of the previous lessons. The mind must be able to resist negative thoughts and desires during the practice of pranayama. Otherwise we may lose our mental equanimity.

If you practice pranayama under proper circumstances then your mind can enter the deeper levels of awareness that first lesson opens up for you.

The first three lessons make the mind calm and steady enough to practice pranayama. Pranayama then brings the vital energy more under our control. While first lesson allows for a degree of concentration, pranayama allows a much deeper concentration and, thus, control of our vital energy.

**Aum:**

It is a popular yogic or new age practice these days to repeat the famous word, Aum (sometimes spelled Om) as a mantra for meditation. However, is Aum an acceptable mantra? Consider the following observations.

Om is properly spelled aum. The 'a' sound is the seed of creation. The 'u' sound indicates "preservation", "maintenance". The 'm' sound, properly written in Sanskrit as 'ma' indicates 'return to the original source.' it is sometimes translated as destruction, which in yogic philosophy would more accurately be called 'transformation'.

Anandamurti says that rather than using aum as a mantra, it is more proper to have it as a goal of your meditation. That is, when your meditation is very deep you will be able to hear the aum sound. This is evidence of advancement in your meditation practice.

The Yoga Sutras of Patanjali, in verse (1:27), support this view, by saying that: "God's voice is Aum."

In the Sikh religion, Guru Nanak writes that, "From Onkar (or Aum), the One Universal Creator God, Brahma was created." He is thus saying that Onkar (Aum) is that which created Brahma and therefore preceded Brahma.

**Fifth Lesson:**

This is called *Chakra Shodhana*. It means purification of the chakras. The section on third lesson explains something of the importance of balanced chakras in our daily and spiritual life. This lesson complements third lesson.

While third lesson emphasizes balancing, controlling and strengthening the chakras, fifth lesson emphasizes the purification of each chakra. The regular practice of this lesson will also spread a spiritual feeling throughout the whole body and the mind.

This lesson is very good for helping us keep our attention in the present moment and it helps the mind to become calm. The practice of keeping attention makes this lesson an important precursor for dhyana, the sixth lesson.

"By keeping the attention in the present moment, we can see more and more clearly the true characteristics of our mind and body process," says Jack Kornfield.

### Sixth Lesson:
"We all have reservoirs of life to draw upon, of which we do not dream."
— William James

The first five lessons of Ananda Marga sadhana prepare our mind, nervous system and body for *dhyana*, meditation. Also, asanas, Yama-Niyama, proper diet, etc., are essential preparation for this practice. Patanjali describes dhyana as unbroken concentration or 'a current of unified thought'. Mastery of the fifth lesson stabilizes the mind, so the necessary concentration of dhyana is possible. It is difficult for a human being to hold a thought unbroken for more than a very few seconds. Even during the brief concentration on this one thought, many other thoughts may try to elbow their way into your consciousness.

Pure meditation, or concentration, then, is no easy matter. However, when it happens, it is a wonderful feeling. We may compare dhyana to pouring oil from one vessel to another, in a steady, unbroken stream. Though we know the oil is flowing, it looks as if it is also standing still. It appears to be a stream that is both moving and motionless. The mind, at the time of dhyana, has perfect steadiness, yet it is moving in a way similar to the flow of oil.

Mircea Eliade, in his classic book, *Yoga*, notes that yogic meditation can take us to, or very close to, understanding the essence of something. He compares this to what he calls 'secular meditation' (which to me seems to describe contemplation or analysis, rather than yogic meditation). In secular meditation, notes Eliade, one can understand the external characteristics of a thing, or perhaps its value. In yogic meditation, though, one can 'penetrate' an object, that is, one can grasp the true essence or nature of something and assimilate it into ones consciousness or experience.

A friend of mine once coined a phrase: "Meditation is not what you think." It is also not what you describe it to be. I cannot compare the deep mental composure and bliss of true meditation to what a person may feel from any music, painting or natural setting. It is way beyond that. Peace or happiness do not describe the results of meditation either. These terms, after all, have a meaning for each of us, depending on our individual nature and characteristics. However, meditation can take us to a spiritual place where we experience a state of not only personal bliss but also a sense of universal unity with all life, with the whole universe.

"Sitting in meditation on my carpet of dust,
I have seen the Supreme Being,
Bathed in the Light that is beyond all light.
Less than the smallest grain,
Greater than all greatness,
Is He -
Him I have found beyond the reaches of sense.
Piercing the veil of my body,
I have seen in sudden flashes
The unquenchable flame."

— Rabindranath Tagore

# Chapter 6

# GURU: THE GUIDE

'The works of artists and men of letters outlive the deeds of businessmen, soldiers and statesmen. The poets and philosophers outrange the historians; while the prophets and saints overtop and outlast them all.'
— Arnold J. Toynbee (*Civilization on Trial*)

'...and it seemed to him that in every joint of every finger of his hand there was knowledge; they spoke, breathed, radiated truth. This man, this Buddha, was truly a holy man...'
— Hermann Hesse (*Siddhartha*)

*Guru*, perfect master, swami: words such as these used to run through my head, leaving an air of mystery, of intrigue, of wonder. At the age of perhaps 18 or 19 I started getting curious about the spiritual life. Early on I heard that a teacher is important. Terms such as guru, perfect master, etc., were tossed around by friends of mine, and were in books that I read and were used by speakers I listened to. Somehow, early on I realized that if one really wants a spiritual guide, then at some time, the right teacher would come. Just call them. But how? And when is one ready to encounter such a guide?

Various stories were going around at that time; stories that may or may not have been true (and some clearly were stories, not reality). As well, some stories that were purported to be true, I would see as parables or exaggerations at best. Both the true stories and the parables whet my appetite for the mystical life and to some extent helped me to understand more about the mystical life.

For example, there was a popular story I heard about Babaji, a mysterious guru in India, who was supposed to have lived for several hundred years. He was hard to find; he didn't publicize himself (nor, I saw later, do other high-caliber gurus) and was known, among other things, for his capacity to travel great distances in very short periods of time.

One story I heard about him concerned a Western man who had been seeking to become a disciple of Babaji for a long time. Somehow he found Babaji (but did he really find Babaji, or rather, was he *allowed* to find Babaji?) in one mountain range of India, where Babaji was staying with some of his disciples.

The Westerner came up to Babaji and asked if he could become his disciple. Babaji refused. The man implored him but he still refused. Finally the man said that if he could not be accepted, he would jump over the nearby cliff to a certain death far below. Still the guru refused, so the man jumped.

As the story goes, his physical body did 'die'. However, Babaji then brought him back to life. The man had, it would seem, passed a very tough test.

I could never confirm that story, but it did have a ring of truth, even if it may not have been completely accurate. The ring of truth was that great sacrifice, a willingness to pass spiritual tests, is part of finding a guru.

Another popular story was clearly a parable. Three men lived on an isolated island. They were constantly engaged in repeating certain prayers and in doing other spiritual exercises. A priest came to the island, saw what they were doing and taught them a prayer from his religion that he assured them was superior to their own practices. They appreciated his teachings. Shortly afterwards the priest left on his boat. As he was crossing the sea he looked back and saw the men pursuing him by walking across the water. They came up to the priest's boat and asked him to repeat the prayer, as they had forgotten how to recite it.

A different type of story concerns Swami Rama, whose book,

*Living with the Himalayan Masters,* is an excellent guide to 20<sup>th</sup> century spiritual India. He is known to have stopped his heart from beating, purely through mental will. This is documented by The Menninger Institute, a reputable medical center in Topeka, Kansas, USA.

So, early on in my spiritual quest, I understood that a teacher – a guru – is important. Even before finding one myself, I understood that these highly evolved beings have extraordinary capabilities. Somehow, it wasn't hard for me to understand that the best teachers don't show off these capabilities, nor do they seek popularity for themselves.

Thus, I accepted that success in meditation depends in part on having the right teacher. The right teacher helps us in almost every aspect of our life.

A child I know is about 16 months old. Walking is still a new experience for her. She can eat a variety of foods, say a few words and understand some of what her mother says to her.

In a way, it's just natural what she is doing, as she takes her first steps on the very long road to growing up. However, virtually everything she knows she has learned with the help of others. The same is true for all of us.

To learn anything we need a teacher. Observe what you do every day. Then analyze how many of those things you learned to do by yourself. Of course there are many things we do without thinking, things that seem to come naturally. However, we had to learn most of what we do from others.

Speaking? This was of course taught, first by hearing people around us speak. A baby has a natural mechanism for picking up language. However, she doesn't pick it up from a vacuum. She needs to hear her parents and others speak.

We learn many other things from example, or directly from others. Tying our shoes, riding a bicycle, driving a car, counting money; these are examples of things that become second nature to many of us. Yet we learned them all from the example or instruction of others.

Most people accept that we do need teachers for these basic things. Nothing, then, should seem more practical than to seek a teacher in order to learn meditation. Most of us do not have meditation or yoga in our background. So a qualified guide is essential.

In yoga the common word for a spiritual teacher is *guru*.

A brief note: The meditation teachers of Ananda Marga are not gurus. We are students of our Guru. As he could not, of course, be everywhere, he trained certain people to represent him world-wide as meditation teachers.

## A Man Who Dared

Swami Vivekananda (1863-1902) was the chief disciple of Shri Ramakrishna. A brilliant student of the Calcutta University and endowed with a questioning mind and a deep philosophical attitude, he went to Shri Ramakrishna to find an answer to the question which was agitating his mind along with that of some of his fellow-students: Was the religion which he had inherited from his forefathers merely a bundle of idolatry and superstition, as the Christian missionaries preached, or did it contain any substance?

As Vivekananda recalled later, when he first called on Shri Ramakrishna, the latter "looked just like an ordinary man, with nothing remarkable about Him".

Could that man be a great leader, Vivekananda wondered and asked Him the question he had asked several others, "Do you believe in God, sir?"

The answer was prompt "Yes".

Vivekananda asked, "Can you prove it, sir?"

Again, the answer was "Yes". Vivekananda then asked

"How?"

Immediately came the answer, "Because I see Him just as I see you here, only in a much more intense sense". That at once impressed Vivekananda.

As He (Swami Vivekananda ) would reminisce later:

For the first time I found a Man who dared to say that He saw God; and that religion was a reality to be felt, to be sensed in an infinitely more intense way than we can sense the world. I began to go to that Man day after day, and I actually saw that religion could be given. One touch, one glance can change a whole life. I have read about Buddha and Christ and Mohammad, about all those different luminaries of ancient times, how They would stand up and say, "Be thou whole", and the man became whole. I now found it to be true, and when I myself saw this Man, all skepticism was brushed aside."

Passage taken from 'Swami Vivekananda – An Anthology' - by Bimal Prasad

---

The word guru is derived from two roots: *Gu* means darkness and *Ru* means to remove. A guru is one who removes darkness or ignorance from the minds of people.

Today the word guru may identify someone who is an expert in some mundane profession. The newspapers may talk about an economics or management or sports guru, for example. The so-called guru is a person who knows a lot about their field of expertise.

However, to be an expert is not the same as to be a teacher. In my university days I found that experts were not always such good teachers. Perhaps because a particular expert is so well versed in their field or because they have little difficulty under-standing the subject, they may not appreciate the difficulties that a 'newcomer' may face. Or perhaps, more simply, they couldn't communicate their formidable knowledge to those who know less.

A good teacher can communicate the necessary knowledge in a clear, comprehensible way, to the students. A guru can do this and also is well versed in that field of knowledge.

Spiritual science is in some ways similar to other fields of learning. It is a body of knowledge that has been gathered and classified through experience and study. Although the benefits of spirituality are available to anyone who seeks them, a guide is necessary to teach us the appropriate techniques. Of course, some gurus are more expert than others. Lower level spiritual gurus may know a lot about the science of yoga, but not be so skilled at transmitting their teachings to their students. As well, lower level gurus may not have achieved much in the way of spirituality themselves. Higher level gurus, however, combine skill and wisdom. I use the word 'skill' here to indicate expertise in practice. Wisdom means an understanding of human nature and an ability to guide us to our deeper, spiritual nature.

I often ask my students what qualifies someone to be a guru. I get many good answers: sincerity, wisdom, love, determination, etc. However, something else – perhaps the most obvious thing – that a guru needs, is a student. This often leads to a discussion of the relationship between the two: does a highly qualified guru always produce good students? Can a lower level guru produce a good student? Can a higher guru produce a bad student? I think that most of these combinations of gurus and students are possible.

A good student is one who is interested in the subject. A good student of yoga makes a special effort to listen to the teachings of the guru. They try their best to assimilate and practice the guru's teachings.

If you are a spiritual aspirant, your relationship with your guru can be one of the most important relationships in your life.

Lama Anagarika Govinda describes his own search in his excellent book, *The Way of the White Clouds*. Coming to Tibet he had been a committed Buddhist for some years. He had had instruction from various teachers, but still felt he lacked a personal guru of a high standard.

During his Tibet travels he had come to understand that a teacher known as 'The Great Lama' (whom he later came to know by the guru's spiritual name, Tomo Geshe Rimpoche) was the guru he sought. However, it was not easy to meet this man. Govinda had to wait a long time before being granted an audience with this Lama.

He writes: "… no matter how long I would have to wait I knew it was worth waiting even for a lifetime to find a real Guru, i.e. one who not only imparted intellectual knowledge but who could awaken the inner forces of one's own mind by the power of his spiritual achievements and realization."

However, how does one know that a guru is qualified? And how does one know that they, as a spiritual seeker, are capable to receive and use the teachings of the guru?

In Tantra several factors contribute to the relationship between guru and student. One is the personal example of the Guru. The student may experience or sense this in personal meetings with the guru. But the Guru does not live forever, so he or she must leave some guidelines and some worthy students behind. These guidelines and students may be considered a heritage; it is what the guru leaves as an example to future generations.

Another factor is the teachings of the guru. A guru may of course comment on any area of life. It is especially useful for a Guru to address certain questions, such as: What is the meaning of life? Why should I do meditation? What is my responsibility to others? Where will this practice lead me? What is the difference between temporary and permanent happiness? What is peace? How can I maintain my health? Besides these, so many other questions can come up.

While answers to such questions are useful, still I may need some other yardstick to measure the quality of a guru, and to decide if they are the best guru for me.

Standard measurements are of course common in the material world. If I buy a car, I take it for a test drive, kick the tires, argue about the price and get some sort of guarantee. I may pay a professional to test the car for me, tell me everything that's wrong with it and what its real market value is.

If I buy some fruit, I can tell if the price matches the quality of the food. With both the car and the fruit, we have no trouble to measure the quality of the item, and decide if the price is right.

With a guru too I also need to know what I'm getting. Price, in terms of money, is irrelevant. True teachers do not ask money from their students to learn spiritual practices. However, our time, commitment and welfare are valuable. So we need a way of knowing what we are getting into.

Long ago Tantric masters developed a checklist of the qualities of a genuine guru.

Some of the qualities include: The guru has self-control, is spiritually evolved, is modest, dresses soberly, has irreproachable conduct, has an honest livelihood, always has pure thoughts, knows spiritual teachings very well, is highly intelligent, is a family person, has the capacity to vitalize and teach proper mantras and is able to give both discipline and love to the students. If you give only discipline or only love to the student you are not taking complete care of them.

Not all these criteria are tangible. Qualities such as being married or having an honest livelihood are clear enough. However, how do you measure 'highly intelligent' or 'spiritually evolved'? It is not easy for the student to judge these things. You, as a prospective student, may need to visit the guru or get to know some of his or her students. What does the guru preach? Does he follow it? Do his closest associates follow these teachings or do they only talk about the teachings? What are the guru's concerns about the world and society? Does he have any opinions or solutions to world problems? Does he have solutions to the personal problems faced by so many people today?

When you can answer these questions, you will have gained an additional insight into the caliber of the guru. One source of the final decision, however, must come from your own heart, from your intuition, your gut feelings about the person. Kahlil Gibran, in his classic book, *The Prophet*, described how to use your inner heart for this:

'And there are those who give and know not pain in giving, nor do they seek joy, nor give with mindfulness of virtue;
They give as in yonder valley the myrtle breathes its fragrance into space.
Through the hands of such as these God speaks, and from behind their eyes He smiles upon the earth.'

Another sort of measurement of Gurus divides them into three types.

The lower type of guru may give some discourses but does not concern himself with the conduct or progress of the disciple. He may take the disciples' offerings but later leave the disciples. He cannot give them any lasting knowledge or practices.

The middle level guru may teach some things and maintain contact with his students. However, he does not lead them to the highest attainment. Perhaps he has not reached the highest spiritual realizations, or perhaps he has no interest or capability to guide the students toward this goal.

The highest level of guru teaches effective practices and takes the necessary steps to ensure that the disciples follow them. He has, of course, all the qualities listed above for a guru, including the fact that he is both strict and loving.

Ideal parents, like an ideal guru, combine discipline and love for their children. If the child feels no love from the parents, it will be hard for him or her to accept their values, except perhaps out of fear. However, even loving parents need to guide the child if s/he is straying from their values. This guidance we may call discipline. A child without a sense of discipline may grow up with little inner strength to make his or her way in the world.

Most parents, of course, have no more than a few children to raise at one time. A guru may have many students, scattered around the world, each with their own particular needs and personalities. Gurus can solve at least part of the problem of personal guidance by giving broad, comprehensive, rational, general guidelines for their followers. They also consider the particular needs of each student. A superior guru guides people on the three levels of spirit, mind and body.

On the spiritual level, the guru has practical and theoretical knowledge. S/he can teach something and explain the teaching. S/he adheres to the principle of "practice what you preach."

On the mental level, s/he is aware of human nature, the needs of the human mind. S/he can remove the sense of want, which so many of us feel in our minds.

On the physical level, s/he understands we all have sorrows and problems, as well as joys. The guru teaches us how to solve the problems of the world. This may include guidance in economics, agriculture, proper diet, health care, ecology and much more.

With my own guru, Anandamurti, I have experienced both the broad and the personal levels of his teachings. He gave his general guidelines in many books and talks. I have adopted these guidelines step by step. I have always found them to be beneficial.

He also demonstrated his personal concern for me on various occasions. One time I was in the Netherlands with him and a hundred or more other people from our group. His daily schedule included a long walk, usually twice a day. He was very busy and often remained inside all day dealing with his many responsibilities. But he took care to get some exercise and fresh air daily, wherever he was.

He always invited a few people to accompany him on his walk and generally engaged them in stimulating, educational conversation. These talks often centered on language, history or society.

One evening I was in the group going on this walk. That day I had a black cloud hanging over me. I felt very frustrated by the events of the day, and as we walked around a large, quiet park, in the descending darkness outside Rotterdam, my mind resounded with one word: "No." Every thought that came into my mind met this one word, which seemed to express my worldview that day. Was I happy to be in Rotterdam? Was I looking forward to the rest of my planned trip around Europe? Did I like the charming, old, narrow house where we were staying? The answer to these and every other question I asked myself was 'No.'

I had not shared my feelings with anyone that day. Indeed, this mood became more intense towards evening and during the walk, which lasted for 30 minutes or more. At the end, we all waited for Anandamurti (also known as Baba to his students) to enter his car with the driver and his attendant, before we got into our cars for the drive back to town.

As he approached me, just before entering his car, he casually asked me if I thought this park was a pleasant place to walk. I answered with a cheerful 'Yes, Baba.' Then, just as he was passing in front of me, he said in a low voice: "Ah, now the boy says yes."

Soon I realized the significance of his remark. I was shocked and amazed. I was also encouraged that my guru was taking care of me. On one level, he was reflecting my feelings back to me as if he was a mirror.

On a deeper level, Anandamurti was telling me that he knew

what was on my mind and in my heart. What he said to me was not a response to my outward behavior.

Soon after this experience, I realized he could pick out any thought or feeling I might have, whether positive or negative. I thought about that, and I talked to others who knew him well and realized that he had no desire to show off his abilities. Please note that his comment to me was quiet, so that only I could hear it. He never referred directly to my negative traits. He did, however, demonstrate that he was aware of my innermost thoughts and in his subtle, silent way, he exhorted me to guide my thoughts to a purer and more positive level.

The relationship between the guru and the student depends a lot on the nature and needs of the student.

There is a famous story about the Tibetan saint, Milarepa who lived in the 11$^{th}$ and 12$^{th}$ centuries. In his youth, he learned black magic to fulfill his mother's wish to destroy the enemies of their family. He later regretted his evil actions. He then searched for a guru to help him overcome his burden of guilt and attain spiritual enlightenment.

With much effort, he found a teacher named Marpa. Marpa knew before Milarepa came that this student had a special destiny. Still, he delayed accepting this young man, to test the student's sincerity. As well, these tests were helping Milarepa to rid himself of the bad karma he had accumulated because of his youthful misdeeds. For a long time Marpa also showered Milarepa with many difficulties which Milarepa could not understand.

A sort of pinnacle of punishment was when Marpa told Milarepa to build a stone house for him. This is not a simple task, nor what Milarepa expected to learn from a spiritual guru. After Milarepa had finished the house Marpa told him he had built it in the wrong place; so Milarepa had to take it apart, stone by stone, and put all the materials back where he had got them. Then he had to start to build a larger house in another place.

Again, after he finished, Marpa told him it was wrong, and again instructed Milarepa to tear it down and build it again in another place. This went on until Milarepa had built the house four times.

To Milarepa this was madness and torture. He underwent much physical and mental suffering before he understood that this trial was for his benefit. When Milarepa came to Marpa he still had heavy karmic debts to repay for the misdeeds of his youth. These actions had of course left a deep impression on his mind. In one way or another, without Milarepa realizing it, these mental impressions or memories of his youthful actions were still guiding his life, even after finding a guru. The intense difficulties his guru gave him helped him to burn out the memories and impressions of these acts of violence. They also helped him to pay off his spiritual debt to the victims of his black magic.

Although Milarepa possessed some very fine qualities, he needed his guru to help him to overcome the mental weaknesses that were holding him back from spiritual growth. The care of the guru, combined with his own efforts and determination, helped to free him from these bondages. His spiritual efforts and accomplishments brought him the highest love and respect from the Tibetan people and from many others around the world.

How does one become a guru? Do you just get married, meditate, dress in simple, clean clothing, study and hope for spiritual wisdom?

There are certain criteria to recognize a Guru, as we have already noted. However, there is no course or syllabus for becoming a guru, as you may have a university course that sets you on the path of becoming a scientist, a business executive or a teacher.

No doubt one needs a deep, unwavering spiritual urge. This seems to build up over lifetimes. As we acquire more spiritual maturity, wisdom and experience, our actions and words attract people to us. I have not heard of any higher-level guru who started his spiritual journey with the idea of becoming a guru. Rather, he started the journey, and continued and persevered on the path, with the goal of knowing the truth about life.

The life of Ramakrishna Paramahansa illustrated this point. As a young man, in the mid-19th century in eastern India, he developed an overriding urge to find the truth. For years he went from temple to temple and teacher to teacher. His efforts rewarded him with deep spiritual wisdom. People started to realize that this man had some special qualities and so his home became the center for a growing number of spiritually thirsty people.

Ramakrishna had not sought these people. They came to him because they recognized his spiritual wisdom and sincerity.

Later he started to think that this wisdom could help humanity and he then began to teach some sincere people what he knew. He then gathered a group of young men who dedicated their lives to spreading his teachings to those people who were hungry for spiritual food.

His most renowned disciple, Swami Vivekananda, first met Ramakrishna when he (Vivekananda), was a student. He was then known as Naren (his family name) and was very intelligent, an excellent singer, idealistic, athletic and handsome. His first impression of Ramakrishna was that this man was strange and he wanted nothing to do with this old yogi. But some intangible force kept drawing him back and Naren's spiritual longing was soon awakened by his connection with Ramakrishna.

Ramakrishna himself was illiterate. However, he could talk with authority on many subjects. This authority came from his heart, from his experience. It did not come from any management courses or psychological manipulation, for within the umbrella of his spiritual knowledge he could find whatever worldly knowledge he needed.

One of Vivekananda's students, Sister Nivedita, describes the Swami's attraction to Ramakrishna. "(In Ramakrishna) was the reality the books only brokenly described... Every moment heard the utterance of wisdom gathered super-consciously... Upon the disciple came the desire for supreme knowledge 'as if it had been a fever'. Yet he who was thus the living embodiment of the books was so unconsciously, for he had read none of them. In his Guru, Ramakrishna, Vivekananda found the key to life."

Every guru has his or her own personality and mode of expression. Some are very scholarly, and explain in minute detail the teachings of ancient texts, while others may arouse their students to a very active life. Is there an underlying connection among all gurus, at least those of the higher levels? I believe that each higher-level guru has a great desire to help everyone reach the goal of life: permanent happiness, fulfillment and a concern and love for all beings in the universe.

As spiritual seekers, you and I face many challenges. For example, our daily life may not encourage or support meditation or the desire for inner awakening. If people see you sitting for a long period with your eyes closed, they may think you are just trying to cut yourself off or to escape from the world. When faced with these questions I explain that my meditation is helping me come in touch with the whole garden of life; I'm learning to see more than the small path in one corner of the garden where I've always walked.

We may face inner doubts as well as outer distractions. I meet meditators who seem to have set some sort of timeline for success in meditation. They seem to think they must make a certain level of progress by a certain date. If not, it means the meditation is not good for them (or that they just can't do it). However, as I suggested earlier, we do not always have the proper tools for measuring our spiritual success or progress. Our training, whether in school or at work, may help us to under-stand that we are gaining certain academic or technical qualifica-tions, but few of us learn in school or at home how to measure spiritual progress. Only experience and persistence will help you to be able to measure spiritual progress.

Overcoming both the inner and outer challenges and difficulties gives us more mental strength. This added strength makes the spiritual journey easier.

## A Breath of Air

There are two traditional stories about gurus, related by Swami Vivekenanda, among others. They are presumably not factual, but still illustrate some of the qualities of a guru.

In the first story, a disciple comes to his spiritual master, his guru, and says, "Sir, I want to know the truth of life." That master looks at the student but says nothing. For several days in a row the disciple comes back and repeats his request. The master gives little or no reply each time.

After some days, it happens to be a hot day and the guru asks the student to come with him to the nearby lake, for a swim. Standing in the lake, the guru pushes the student under the water and holds him down there for a long time, even as the student struggles madly to come up. Then the guru lets him up and asks him: "What did you want more than anything when you were under water?" The disciple says: "A breath of air!"

The guru responds: "When you want God, just as you wanted a breath of air, you will have God very soon."

Another traditional story tells of a great king who was hunting in the forest and met a sage. After a talk with the sage, the king was so pleased with the man's wisdom that he asks him to accept a present from himself, the king.

The sage replies that he is most satisfied here in the forest, as he has fruits to eat from the trees, water in the river, a place to sleep and nothing is needed that he cannot find in the forest.

A long discussion ensued, and finally the king persuaded the sage to come with him to the city, to receive a present from him.

Arriving at the king's palace the sage saw worldly wealth and power as one could hardly find anywhere else on earth, in the forms of gold, jewelry, marble, beautiful gardens, finely dressed people and so much else.

The king then asked the sage to wait briefly while he said his daily prayers. The sage heard the king praying for more wealth, more healthy children, more territory, etc.

At this, the sage started to leave the palace. Soon the king finished his prayers and rushed after the sage. "Sir," said the king, "you did not take any present from me. Where are you going?!"

The sage replied: "I do not need to receive presents from a beggar, which I now understand you to be."

People sometimes tell me it seems very hard to find a guru, a proper teacher. Is the guru hiding for some reason? No, though it may seem that way. However, though the guru is always there, you may need to take a few steps on the spiritual path in order to see him or her. Perhaps s/he is just waiting for the right moment in your life. When you view a forest from the distance, it may appear as if all the trees are the same, but when we start walking in the forest, we can see a wide variety of trees. We can also see the flowers which blossom in the midst of the forest. Just as we do not see the flowers till we enter the forest, so we may not see – or recognize – the guru until we have started to walk along the spiritual path.

Your own spiritual evolution and desire, along with a sense of discrimination, help you find a suitable guru. There is an old saying in India: "If a pickpocket meets a saint, he'll just see his pockets." Conversely, the saint upon meeting the pickpocket will see the possible good in the thief. In such a situation, a wise saint will also keep his hand near his wallet. However, he will not try to pigeonhole the person as a pickpocket. This only reinforces the pickpocket's self-image, making it harder for him to leave this line of work. An exceptional saint may be able to awaken the spiritual desire in the thief.

Anandamurti was in this situation once, as a university student in Calcutta. His spiritual journey had shown him much about life, about the true needs and desires of humanity. However, he had not yet started teaching yoga.

One day he was walking in a quiet area on the bank of the Hooghly River in Calcutta. Sunset approached and he was sitting alone, lost in his thoughts. Soon he felt a dark, foreboding presence. Looking around he saw a large, menacing man with a knife. The man demanded his money.

Anandamurti sat there silently. Then, as if talking to an old friend, he said: "What is it you really want Kalicharan?" The man, Kalicharan Bannerjee, was a notorious robber and murderer. He could not understand how this slight young gentleman knew his name. Why was this youth not quivering in fear? Why did he sit undisturbed, talking to him in such a natural way?

The voice, words and demeanor of Anandamurti struck some chord in a deep recess of Kalicharan's mind. Anandamurti beckoned Kalicharan to come and sit by him. In a short time he helped Kalicharan to understand that he had much more to do in this life than steal and kill. Soon Kalicharan asked Anandamurti to help him find spiritual realization. He took a sort of Tantric baptism by bathing in the river and afterwards Anandamurti taught him meditation.

Kalicharan, later known as Kalikananda Avadhuta, began his spiritual quest in the presence of his guru. Most of us do not find such an immediate connection. Not long after I began my search for spiritual realization, I also realized I should have a teacher, a guru who could guide me on this quest. As this desire became stronger, I came into more and more contact with gurus and their disciples or followers.

Some followers seemed to esteem their gurus as little more than spiritual pop stars. I tended to give a wide berth to these followers and, for better or worse, to their gurus. Mike, for example, was a friend of mine during our university days. He was at that time a suave, glib, upper-middle class hippie. Later he met a guru and became a suave, glib, upper-middle class devotee. I had several conversations with Mike about his guru. Mike's rap about his guru could be summarized as follows: "He is the one and only guru. The best. You must follow him now." With this attitude, Mike kept me and others from developing any interest in meeting his guru.

In those days I had just a dim idea of what to look for in a guru. I did know, though, that your guru will find you, if you are open-minded and desirous to meet him or her. So I kept looking and trying to send out signals that would let my guru know I was there.

Although I could not well articulate what type of person I was looking for, I did have an idea that this person would have some qualities that put him or her above the run of the mill teacher. Some books I had read gave me the feeling I should look for one who was humble, inwardly strong, modest, respectful, compassionate and principled. I could not, however, articulate these points. So, though I didn't approach prospective gurus with a checklist, I knew in my heart that I was not looking for a superficial person. During my search I was fortunate to meet many interesting people who often taught me valuable lessons about spirituality and the guru.

One 'non-guru' helped me a lot. Ram Dass, born as Richard Alpert, was a Harvard psychiatrist who later matriculated to

LSD with his more famous colleague, Timothy Leary. Alpert eventually dropped out of that curriculum and found a guru in India. He came back to the USA and wrote books and lectured about the various aspects of his spiritual growth. His main message, as I understood, was that with any material 'high', whether LSD, money, fame, sex, etc., you always come down, no matter how far up you go. With meditation, though, you can get higher and higher and no fall is necessary. What you need is the right path. When you find the right guru you find the right path.

I also met a teacher named Pir Vilayat Khan. A Sufi exponent and son of a respected Sufi master, he was a well-known figure on the new age circuit in the USA. Articulate and soft-spoken, he seemed, to me, to talk from experience and with compassion.

Once after a lecture of his I approached him with one simple, brash question: "Sir, have you ever had samadhi?" He was silent and seemed to search some remote corner of the room for an answer. He then looked at me, pressed my arm sharply and said: "Everybody feels something." My thank you to him hid an inner grumble at what seemed a non-answer. Much later I realized samadhi is not as tangible as a frosty beer on a hot summer day, or a job promotion with a hefty raise. When I understood this I appreciated his answer. I also realized that if he had told me 'yes,' it could have seemed egoistic. If he'd told me no, I may have been deflated. So he told me the truth, leaving his personality out of his answer.

Some time later I attended a talk by an august, famous Indian swami in San Francisco. The ads and promotional literature raised him to great heights. His holy demeanor was, I felt, far too weighty an affair for me. However, it seemed the opulence of his lifestyle was appropriate for some people.

Later I met Mr. M.P. Pandit, a close disciple of the late Sri Aurobindo, a Bengali social revolutionary against the British occupation in India, who later became a renowned mystic and poet. Mr. Pandit was down to earth, enchanting, practical and wise. He urged us to adopt the spiritual path, but also the path of social responsibility and social change. Optimism about the future, along with an attitude of vigor, sincerity and discipline were at the core of his message.

I went up to talk to him after his lecture. I waited as he finished a discussion with an older Indian gentleman of his own generation. The man grumbled that although Sri Aurobindo's ideas were no doubt good, one shouldn't move too fast. It was not the time now for much change. Yoga and meditation are enough, the man insisted. Mr. Pandit smiled at him and urged him on his way with a polite but firm good-bye. He then turned to me, who was a bit more than a third of his own age, and said: "See, those old folks will never do anything. It's you young people who will change the world."

I gained much from meeting these teachers, and many more like them. However, if I had kept searching and searching, without at least trying out one path, my search would have become a bit like window-shopping. You'll never know how good those shoes in the window are, unless you get the right size, try them on, pay the clerk and walk a few mountains in them. Even when you've decided to try out one spiritual path, it may take some time, climbing a few inner mountains, to know if the path and guru are for you.

If your mind is open and perceptive, you'll gain something even from the wrong guru. Then you can just move on, with sincerity, eagerness and humility, continuing your search for the right path.

When I first heard about Ananda Marga, which later became my chosen spiritual path, I thought of it as just another name in a growing pool of modern mystical movements. A brother of a friend mentioned it, later a friend of a friend and here and there I heard another word or two about Ananda Marga.

I had several reservations about most of the groups I had met or heard about. They all seemed somewhat removed from the daily reality of life. They did not seem to answer many practical questions. How can I pay my bills, find a job, find friends and lovers and end the needless suffering in the world? Most of these groups seemed to promise a metaphysical Shangri-la, but only for me as an individual, or for the inner circle of its members. This type of promise did not appeal to me. I felt it was irrational and selfish.

One day I decided to go to a lecture in the town of Carbondale, about five hours drive away. Ram Dass (mentioned above), who I had met a couple of years earlier, was talking. So I caught a ride with a friend and off we went. It turned out he and his other friends in the car were all members of Ananda Marga. Oh, I thought, okay, no problem. I also learned that Ananda Marga was sponsoring the Ram Dass evening.

When we reached Carbondale, we went to the Ananda Marga center before the lecture. I learned that this evening with Ram Dass was a fundraiser for some Ananda Marga projects. They were running a hostel for unwed mothers. They were also teaching meditation classes in a federal prison near Carbondale. It was the maximum-security prison in the United States, which had some years earlier replaced the more famous Alcatraz.

Their ideas attracted me. Meditation to make me happier, more at peace and more in control of my life and using the benefits of meditation to help others. These people are not just sitting at home all day chanting and praying; they also go out and engage themselves in the world.

That evening I also learned that the guru, Anandamurti, had just started a protest fast in prison in his native India. Why was he in prison, I wondered. Didn't he pay his taxes? No, something quite different. Ananda Marga was in hot water with the national government and some state governments in India. Ananda Marga had an egalitarian social philosophy that pinched the nerves of both the communist and capitalist interests in India. Ananda Marga also stressed honesty and morality, which was even more of a pinch to many vested interests in India. For example, one Ananda Marga member, a senior customs officer, had arrested the wealthy son of a well-known politician. The man, like many in his class, was smuggling a large amount of valuable goods into India. His arrest shocked the upper classes in India since they were used to paying bribes rather than taxes.

So, one thing led to another, and Anandamurti was arrested on false charges (the false nature of the charges was later proved in court). By the time I learned about all this in Carbondale, he had been in prison for more than a year. His fast was a protest against the government mistreatment of him and his followers.

Now, at this early date in my relationship with Ananda Marga I could not tell if the Ananda Marga version of the story was true. However, I kept meeting Ananda Marga members and I read a little about their philosophy.

I thought I would check them out more in my hometown. I did and I liked what I saw.

About two months later I met a teacher, an *acharya*, of Ananda Marga and asked him to initiate me. I had been practicing a simple, popular technique of 'meditation' for about two years. However, when I learned Ananda Marga meditation from the acharya, I felt I was entering a deeper, more substantial level of spiritual practice. I never looked back.

A word about what an acharya is. In Ananda Marga, an acharya teaches the meditation techniques and guides the members in their spiritual practices and social conduct. The word acharya means, "one who teaches by example." Anandamurti also notes that an acharya is "a person who utilizes his or her intellect for the benefit of others."

In any spiritual system the guru is the real teacher and guide. However, the guru cannot be everywhere. The many people who want to learn about meditation and related practices cannot always come to meet the guru, who may live far away. The guru, likewise, may not have the time to give personal instruction in meditation and the related practices to every interested person.

So, Anandamurti solved this problem by training certain of his disciples to teach on his behalf. In the early days, Anandamurti alone taught his students. Later on he trained teachers, who travelled throughout India teaching the spiritual practices of Ananda Marga.

In those days, all the acharyas were family people. The first group he trained consisted of three men and two women. This group expanded year by year. By the early 1960s Ananda Marga was increasing its activities around India, and the family people started to find it difficult to give the amount of time required, as they also had to go to work and take care of their family responsibilities. So Anandamurti began training some of his students to be monks and nuns who could leave their worldly responsibilities and work full time to impart the knowledge of how to attain 'ananda' — spiritual fulfillment — to the general population.

Today most of the acharyas in Ananda Marga are monks and nuns (*sannyasis* in Sanskrit). There are still a fair amount of family acharyas. Most of them are in India, maintaining the balance between their family lives and their duties as spiritual guides to the community. A Sannyasi, in the tradition of Tantra, is one who, "out of noble intentions and benevolent outlook, has sacrificed his or her personal life to find the highest truths and to help others to overcome all their difficulties in life as they strive to do the same."

Learning meditation is not just a mechanical process. Genuine initiation into meditation involves a subtle energy transfer from the guru to the initiate. The acharya acts as a conduit between the two. As the acharya needs to be a proper conduit, so the student needs to be a proper receptacle.

The purity, or 'conductivity', of an acharya depends on their exemplary conduct, as well as on their understanding of how to teach the meditation techniques. Anandamurti notes: "An acharya shall always instruct by his or her exemplary actions and words." If he or she is following Yama and Niyama correctly, this gives them the necessary spiritual purity to be able to transfer the spiritual energy from the guru to the student.

Earlier we talked about the lessons of meditation. A word about initiation is relevant here.

Initiation is not just a mechanical process, where the acharya sits with you and tells you how to repeat a mantra. A mantra is not just a word you repeat to relax from life's stresses. It is a sound that has been empowered with spiritual energy from a guru.

Lama Anagarika Govinda notes that, '... a Guru is able to perform the rites of initiation and the transference of power only if he has generated this power within himself through years of hard training — and even then he will generally spend many days and nights in deep meditation before performing any of these rites.'

The essence or root of meditation is a mantra. We've discussed this earlier. How, though, does a guru make a mantra? How do they energize certain sounds so that they have a spiritually vital effect on the meditator?

We all know that sounds affect us. The loud barking of a dog, for example, will create a feeling of tension or fear in most people. On the other hand, certain types of music will have a soothing affect on us. A great musician knows what combination of notes and rhythm will produce what affect on listeners and they combine intelligence and intuition to put these sounds together in their music.

A guru also uses intelligence and intuition to create a mantra. When a guru takes his or her subtle consciousness to a high level during deep meditation, then s/he can energize the sounds. The sounds then become mantras. When the mantra is properly transmitted, it will awaken the 'sleeping' spiritual energy in the student. Although the spiritual energy is awakened by the process of initiation, it may not go anywhere, unless the student practices meditation. If the student does practice the meditation, then the spiritual energy can move upwards.

Dr. Patricia Carrington says: 'When intoned under proper conditions, a mantra can awaken the dormant energy of an individual, his unique wave pattern, his bija. Recognizing this unique pattern in a disciple, the guru must draw on his own direct realization of the mantra in order to intone the exact frequency which will ignite the intrinsic power coiled up in that mantra and in that individual.'

She continues: 'A close relationship between master and pupil forms the basis for the assignment of a mantra by a guru to suit his particular student.'

Most of us need direct physical contact with our teacher. We cannot learn meditation through intuition or books. Thus the acharyas, as conduits for the guru, become the guru's representatives.

Certain aspects of the initiation process help the pupil to attain a closer direct, spiritual connection with the guru. This is explained at the time of initiation.

Since the guru's personality is involved in the mantra they have empowered, the guru transmits something of him or herself to the student also. Regular meditation can help the student to perceive certain ideas or energies that emanate from the guru, regardless of any physical distance from the guru.

An important part of the initiation is that the student is able to establish a link with the guru by making a spiritual offering to the guru. This offering takes nothing from you. Rather, as Robert South notes: "If there be any truer measure of a person than by what he or she does, it must be by what they give."

Meditation is a special process that helps us increase what we have, in terms of vitality, knowledge and overall sense of fulfillment in life. These qualities are not things that can be taken away from us. And strangely, the more we give of these qualities, the more we seem to have inside us.

As a final note, Anandamurti often reminded us that the practices we are doing are not only known as meditation. We said earlier that he preferred to use the word 'sadhana.' Sadhana is an effort to complete a task. The sixth lesson of our meditation course is called *dhyana*, which literally means meditation. I believe a sincere student of meditation, of yoga, of Tantra, will find many rewards along the way. However, it is my experience that these rewards are far removed from the modern concept of a reward. They don't always come to you when you expect them, nor when you demand them.

"There are pearls in the deep sea, but one must hazard all to find them. If diving once does not bring you pearls, you need not therefore conclude that the sea is without them. Dive again and again. You are sure to be rewarded in the end."

— Ramakrishna Paramahansa

# BOOKS

## MySpiritRadio

There are many valid, reasons why people start to meditate. The experiences of Dada Jyotirupananda tell him that if you persist with a meditation practice, you'll sooner or later seek answers to the deeper questions even if you didn't start to meditate for any spiritual or esoteric reason.

This book will provide you with tools that can help you to meditate and will help you gain a stronger commitment to regular meditation practice. Learn about how to meditate, about yoga exercises and related practices. Learn how to be healthy through your own efforts and how to adopt a code of conduct that will see you through life's difficulties, and will help guide you to the deepest fulfilment.

*Jyotirupananda helps us rethink our craft, and, with fine learning and authorship, leads us to a new understanding of what meditation might really mean in our lives and the benefits we might reap from it.*
Ross Heaven, author of *Love's Simple Truths: Meditations on Rumi*

Dada Jyotirupananda has practiced meditation since 1971, and has been a meditation teacher since 1985. He has taught meditation in about 25 countries.

BOOKS

Body, Mind & Spirit
UK £11.99
US $24.95

www.o-books.net
Cover design by Design Deluxe

US $24.95
ISBN 978-1-84694-219-8

9 781846 942198